The

WITHDRAWN
Speedway Public Library

Reference

Shelf

Representative American Speeches 2000–2001

Editors

Calvin M. Logue, Ph.D.

and

Lynn M. Messina, Ph.D.

The Reference Shelf
Volume 73 • Number 6

The H.W. Wilson Company
2001

The Reference Shelf

The books in this series contain reprints of articles, excerpts from books, addresses on current issues, and studies of social trends in the United States and other countries. There are six separately bound numbers in each volume, all of which are usually published in the same calendar year. Numbers one through five are each devoted to a single subject, providing background information and discussion from various points of view and concluding with a subject index and comprehensive bibliography that lists books, pamphlets, and abstracts of additional articles on the subject. The final number of each volume is a collection of recent speeches, and it contains a cumulative speaker index. Books in the series may be purchased individually or on subscription.

Library of Congress has cataloged this serial title as follows:

Representative American speeches. 1937 / 38–
    New York, H. W. Wilson Co.
        v. 21 cm.—The Reference Shelf
Annual
Indexes:
        Author index: 1937/38–1959/60, with 1959/60;
        1960/61–1969/70, with 1969/70; 1970/71–1979/80,
        with 1979/80; 1980/81–1989/90, 1990.
        Editors: 1937/38–1958/59, A. C. Baird.—1959/60–1969/70, L. Thonssen.—1970/71–
1979/80, W. W. Braden.—1980/81–1994/95, O. Peterson.—1995/96–1998/99 , C. M. Logue
and J. DeHart.—1999/2000– , C. M. Logue and L. M. Messina.
        ISSN 0197-6923 Representative American speeches.
        1. Speeches, addresses, etc., American. 2. Speeches, addresses, etc.
        I. Baird, Albert Craig, 1883–1979 ed. II. Thonssen, Lester, 1904–
        III. Braden, Waldo Warder, 1911–1991 ed.
        IV. Peterson, Owen, 1924– ed. V. Logue, Calvin McLeod, 1935– , Messina, Lynn M.,
        and DeHart, Jean, eds. VI. Series.
PS668.B3   815.5082   38-27962
                                                          MARC-S

Library of Congress [8503r85] rev4

Cover:

Visit H.W. Wilson's Web site: www.hwwilson.com

Printed in the United States of America

CONTENTS

Preface

The year 2000 ended with the United States embroiled in one of the most contentious presidential elections in its history. Polls had indicated that Americans were split almost exactly down the middle in their support for the Republican candidate George W. Bush and the Democratic Vice President Al Gore. At the end of Election Day on November 7, the state of Florida was too close to call, and by the next day, a recount was underway in that state. The next six weeks included revelations of ballot irregularities and confusion in Florida and other states; lawsuits filed by each candidate's party; decisions on manual recounts by the Federal District Court and Florida State Supreme Court; accusations by Democrats of bias on the part of Florida's Republican administration; and finally, a 5–4 decision by the United States Supreme Court ending the manual recount and awarding Florida's 25 electoral votes to Bush, who had lost the nation's popular vote to Gore.

Once the new president took office, the popular issues of the day returned to the fore, including education, a possible energy crisis, and the increasing ethnic diversity revealed in the 2000 census—topics addressed in several of the speeches contained in this book. Nevertheless, the fallout from the 2000 election could be felt for months afterwards, affecting the way many Americans looked at the presidency, the election process, and the role of the judiciary. Because the year 2000 ended and 2001 began with the election results at the front of so many people's minds, the first two chapters of this book include several speeches on that subject.

In the first chapter, "The American Justice System," U.S. Supreme Court Justice Ruth Bader Ginsburg—who wrote one of the four dissenting opinions in *Bush v. Gore*—and Mary J. Mullarkey, Chief Justice of Colorado's Supreme Court, consider the issue of judicial independence, especially in light of the attacks leveled against judges deciding cases related to the 2000 election. Ohio Chief Justice Thomas J. Moyer and Bill Lann Lee also speak about fairness in the courts, particularly as it bears upon the issues of economic and racial bias.

Chapter II, "Election Reform," includes speeches by Julia Hughes Jones, who worries about the potential, in our electronic age, of interested parties manipulating voting results and "stealing" elections, as well as Carolyn Jefferson-Jenkins of the League of Women Voters, who argues that voting restrictions may be preventing far too many Americans from fully participating in the democratic process. Scott Harshbarger of Common Cause expresses concerns about the use of outdated voting machines, difficulties in voter registration, and the role of the Electoral College in deciding the president. The final two speeches then present both sides of the debate concerning campaign finance reform, with Senator John McCain advocating strict limitations on campaign spending, and Senator Mitch McConnell arguing that such limitations infringe upon the First Amendment.

The speakers in the next chapter, "Education," reflect upon an issue of continuing concern for Americans today. While Liam E. McGee asserts that education reform is in the interest of the business community, Richard A. Gephardt of the House of Representatives reviews the challenges facing America's public schools, including crowded classrooms, teacher shortages, and student safety. Michele Cavataio Sacconaghi of AOL Time Warner describes the possibilities for using computers in the classroom, and John B. Donovan speaks of the spiritual and ethical benefits to children who participate in Release Time religious education. Author and education expert Alfie Kohn next considers the damaging effects of standardized tests on elementary and high school students, while Lawrence W. Reed argues for school choice through tax credits to parents, rather than the more controversial voucher plan.

Chapter IV, "Diversity," examines the complexities of one of America's greatest strengths. Antoinette M. Bailey uses the example of bio-diversity to argue the need for greater ethnic and gender diversity in American business. In a campaign speech, Pat Buchanan next proposes severe limits on immigration to America so as to better assimilate those immigrants who are already here. While Dr. Albert C. Yates of Colorado State University reviews the struggles faced by an ethnically diverse society, Rabbi Steven Lebow considers the heroism of average Americans of different racial, economic, and social backgrounds whose daily work contributes to the fabric of the nation.

The final chapter in the book, called simply "Energy," addresses a subject on the lips of many Americans during 2000–2001—the possibility of a nationwide energy crisis. A speech by Kathleen Hogan of the Environmental Protection Agency expresses concerns about America's inordinate reliance on fossil fuel and the prospect of turning to more efficient sources of energy. Former U.S. Secretary of Energy Bill Richardson next addresses the energy story of the year, California's electricity shortage, which resulted in sharp price increases and rolling blackouts. By the Spring of 2001, lawmakers like Senator Frank H. Murkowski of Alaska, whose speech follows, were arguing for limited oil and gas drilling in the Arctic National Wildlife Refuge. This proposal was supported by the next speaker represented here, Vice President Dick Cheney, who asserts that conservation is not a sound energy policy. The final speech in the book by the Nuclear Regulatory Commissioner, Jeffrey S. Merrifield, discusses preparations for licensing additional nuclear reactors, which many believe could help America to meet its present and future energy demands.

December 2001

I. The American Justice System

Remarks on Judicial Independence

The Situation of the U.S. Federal Judiciary[1]

Ruth Bader Ginsburg

Associate Justice of the U.S. Supreme Court, 1993– ; born Brooklyn, NY, March 15, 1933; Phi Beta Kappa, Phi Kappa Phi, B.A., in Government, Cornell University, 1954; attended Harvard Law School, 1956–58, Harvard Law Review; *LL.B. (J.D.), Columbia Law School,* Columbia Law Review *and Kent Scholar, 1959; admitted to New York Bar, 1959, and District of Columbia Bar, 1975; Founder and Counsel, Women's Rights Project, American Civil Liberties Union, 1972–80, and General Counsel to that project, 1973–80; Professor, Rutgers University School of Law, 1963–72; Professor, Columbia Law School, 1972–80; Fellow, Center for Advanced Study in the Behavioural Sciences, Stanford, California, 1977–78; U.S. Court of Appeals for the District of Columbia Circuit, 1980–93; authored (with Anders Bruzelius)* Civil Procedure in Sweden, *1965;* Text, Cases, and Materials on Sex-Based Discrimination *(with Herma Hill Kay and Kenneth M. Davidson), 1974; numerous articles on civil procedure, conflict of laws, constitutional law, and comparative law; board member, American Bar Association Journal and American Bar Foundation; council member, American Law Institute; member of the Council on Foreign Relations and the American Academy of Arts and Sciences; honorary degrees from twenty-two colleges and universities.*

Editors' introduction: Associate Justice Ginsburg addressed more than 300 law faculty, teachers, students, and members of the bench and bar attending The Rule of Law Public Address Series in the University of Melbourne auditorium. Professor Cheryl Saunders, Director of the series, noted that the addresses were "timed to coincide with the centenary of the Australian Constitution in 2001." Saunders explained further that the series was meant to address the challenges and tensions arising from attempts by various national and international bodies to understand and apply the "doctrine of the rule of law." Associate

---

1. Delivered on February 1, 2001, at Melbourne, Victoria, Australia, in the early evening prior to a dinner. Reprinted with permission of Ruth Bader Ginsburg. Justice Ginsburg acknowledges with appreciation the grand assistance of her 2000 Term law clerk, Goodwin Liu, in composing these remarks.

Justice Ginsburg's speech was to be the only one given by a citizen of the United States.

Ruth Bader Ginsburg's speech: I am pleased to be among the speakers invited to participate in this well-timed series on The Rule of Law. The theme was chosen, Professor Cheryl Saunders wrote in her November 1999 invitation letter, in part for its link with judicial independence. I presented a talk on that topic at a February 1998 Hawaii State Bar Reception. Soon thereafter, at the suggestion of Justice Michael Kirby of Australia's High Court, *The Australian Law Journal* sought permission to reprint my Hawaii remarks. I was glad to say yes, more so when it turned out that the *Australian Law Journal* was as prompt as the *Hawaii Law Review* was tardy. I had the offprints from Australia in hand months before the Hawaii journal emerged from the press.[1]

> *My aim . . . is to offer some thoughts . . . on just how important—and difficult—it is for judges to do what is legally right, no matter what "the home crowd" wants.*

Professor Saunders thought an elaboration of my remarks on judicial independence, from the United States perspective, would be of interest to this audience. The revision of my 1998 presentation was just about done at the start of December when a case called *Bush v. Gore* came before the United States Supreme Court. Days later, at 10 p.m. on December 12, 2000, the Court released a 5-4 decision that made headlines round the world.[2] I have adjusted this presentation to take account of that breathtaking episode.

Of all the words recently spoken and written about judicial independence in the United States—and whatever one makes of the U.S. Supreme Court's part in calling the excruciatingly close November 2000 election for President Bush—a 1980 comment by the U.S. Chief Justice remains, in my view, right on target. On the obligation of a good judge, Chief Justice Rehnquist then said: He or she must strive constantly to do what is legally right, all the more so when the result is not the one the Congress, the President, or "the home crowd" wants.[3] My aim in this lecture is to offer some thoughts, from the vantage point of a U.S. federal judge, on just how important—and difficult—it is for judges to do what is legally right, no matter what "the home crowd" wants.

I.

If it is true, as Henry Fielding wrote, that examples work more forcibly on the mind than precepts,[4] then allow me to begin with a few trying cases, situations in which the U.S. Supreme Court intervened to resolve controversies some thought best left to political decision-makers—to the Executive or the Congress. My first two illustrations today generate no sparks in the United States. The third awaits history's judgment.

I will recall first a 1974 case titled *United States v. Nixon*,[5] which yielded a unanimous opinion written by Chief Justice Rehnquist's predecessor, Warren Burger. On Chief Justice Burger's death, a *New York Times* obituary praised the opinion as "the pinnacle of [Burger's] career and one of the [U.S.] judiciary's finest achievements."[6] The case concerned a subpoena issued by U.S. District Judge John Sirica at the height of the Watergate scandal. Judge Sirica's subpoena directed the President to produce, for use in a criminal proceeding, tape recordings and documents capturing Oval Office conversations between Nixon and his closest advisers.

In his campaigns for the presidency, Nixon had repeatedly called for the restoration of "law and order." He promised to appoint judges equal to the task, people who would not be "soft on crime."[7] A United States Supreme Court that included four Nixon appointees, including Chief Justice Burger and now Chief Justice Rehnquist, declared the law and affirmed Judge Sirica's order. The President obeyed, then promptly resigned from office.

Earlier in time, my second illustration is popularly known as the "steel seizure case," *Youngstown Sheet & Tube Co. v. Sawyer*.[8] In the spring of 1952, the United States was heavily engaged in the Korean War. At home, inflation was rising, and labor unrest was widespread. For several months, the United Steel Workers of America had been seeking a substantial wage increase, which the steel companies had repeatedly refused. With negotiations at an impasse, the steel workers voted to strike beginning on April 9. On the evening of April 8, to keep the mills in operation, President Truman issued an executive order directing the Secretary of Commerce to take possession of 85 steel companies. The order declared that "a work stoppage would immediately jeopardize and imperil our national defense . . . and would add to the continuing danger of our soldiers, sailors, and airmen engaged in combat in the field."[9]

The steel companies argued that the order was an unconstitutional encroachment on congressional authority. In response, the government urged that a strike would so endanger the well-being and safety of the Nation that the President must be held to possess "inherent power" to seize the steel mills. The United States District Court in Washington, D.C., rejected the government's plea and enjoined enforcement of the President's order. But the full Court of Appeals immediately voted 5-4 to stay the district court injunction, with the eight judges appointed by Truman evenly divided on the issue. One month later, a 6-3 majority of the United States Supreme Court declared the President's order invalid; the authority to seize property, the Court held, is a lawmaking power which the Constitution vests in Congress alone "in both good and bad times."[10]

While four of the Justices in the majority were appointed by Truman's predecessor, Franklin Roosevelt, the fifth and sixth votes came from Justices Burton and Clark, both Truman appointees. In a concurring opinion, Justice Clark explained (borrowing words written by Justice Story more than a century earlier) that, although the Court gives "the most entire respect" to the executive branch, "[i]t is our duty to expound the laws as we find them in the records of state; and we cannot, when called upon by the citizens of the country, refuse our opinion, however it may differ from that of very great authorities."[11] President Truman immediately complied with the Court's judgment. "[L]ess than thirty minutes after the Justices finished reading their opinions," he dispatched a letter ordering the Secretary of Commerce to return the confiscated mills to their owners.[12]

More than 150 years ago, a young French observer of democracy in America, Alexis de Tocqueville, made this prescient comment: "Scarcely any political question arises in the United States that is not resolved, sooner or later, into a judicial one."[13] Were the Watergate and steel seizure cases not enough to illustrate Tocqueville's insight, my third example, *Bush v. Gore*,[14] surely provides graphic confirmation of its truth. The Court's decision in that case ended 36 days of controversy over the 2000 presidential election.

The petition for review in *Bush v. Gore* was filed in the United States Supreme Court on the evening of December 8, 2000, hours after the Florida Supreme Court had ordered statewide manual recounts of certain disputed ballots. Whether the recounting was permissible under state and federal law raised questions whose stakes could not have been higher. On December 8, George W. Bush led Al Gore in the Florida vote tally by some hundreds of votes—a razor-thin margin in an election with over 6 million votes cast statewide. At the national level, Gore had won the popular vote, and with 267 all-important electoral votes compared to Bush's 246, Gore was only three electoral votes shy of victory under the presidential electoral system decreed by the U.S. Constitution. The winner of Florida's popular election would capture all of the State's 25 decisive electoral votes and, in turn, the Presidency.

One would expect that the first instinct of any judge, faced with such a case, would be restraint. The Supreme Court's initial encounter with the controversy might fit that description. Just five days before it agreed to hear *Bush v. Gore*, the Supreme Court issued a unanimous decision declining to intervene at an earlier point in the unfolding drama, when the Florida Supreme Court had interpreted Florida election laws to allow manual recounts to go forward in certain counties.[15] The U.S. Supreme Court found the underpinnings of the Florida Supreme Court's initial decision unclear, and therefore remanded the case for clarification whether federal law had been duly considered. In that measured response, the U.S. Supreme Court referred to precedent counseling restraint when "there is considerable uncertainty as to the precise grounds of [a state court] decision."[16]

Not since 1876 had a presidential contest been so close, and not since then had the Nation waited so long for a definitive resolution.

In the ensuing irresolution, pressure on the political and legal system continued to mount. Not since 1876 had a presidential contest been so close, and not since then had the Nation waited so long for a definitive resolution. On December 9, one day after the Florida Supreme Court's decision ordering statewide manual recounts, the pressure pushed the unanimity of the United States Supreme Court past its breaking point, as a 5-4 majority voted to stay the recounts pending review and disposition of *Bush v. Gore*.[17]

Ordinarily, interim stay orders of the Court, like grants of review, issue without explanation. But this was no ordinary case. Justice Stevens took the unusual step of issuing a written dissent, which Justice Souter, Justice Breyer, and I joined, stating reasons for concluding that the stay was unjustified.[18] In the dissenters' view, the Court should have stayed out of the fray entirely, leaving its ultimate resolution to Congress. Justice Scalia took the even more unusual step of explaining why he voted in favor of a stay securing Court adjudication of the controversy.[19] Each side warned that the other risked casting a cloud of illegitimacy over the election.[20]

On December 12, three days after granting review, and one day after oral argument, the U.S. Supreme Court released its decision. Unaccompanied by the usual syllabus, and including six separate writings, the release first confused instant reporters. The outcome, however, is by now clear to all. In an unsigned opinion, five Justices agreed that under the Equal Protection Clause of the U.S. Constitution, the Florida Election Code's "intent of the voter" standard provided insufficient guidance for manually recounting disputed ballots.[21] The five Justices further agreed that there was no time left to conduct recounts under constitutionally acceptable standards.[22] That was so, the per curiam opinion explained, because the Florida Supreme Court had interpreted Florida election law to require completion of all vote counts by December 12, the date by which, under federal law, Florida had to certify its election results in order to gain for the State's electoral votes "conclusive" effect in Congress' tally of all electoral votes.[23]

> *The wisdom of the Court's decision to intervene [in Bush v. Gore], and the wisdom of its ultimate determination . . . await history's judgment.*

Four Justices dissented. Two said that the "intent of the voter" standard presented equal protection concerns, but also said that those concerns might be met on remand.[24] Two determined that the standard raised no equal protection problem, particularly in view of the range of local voting systems and ballot designs traditionally tolerated.[25] (I was one of those two.) All four dissenting Justices agreed that the December 12 deadline was illusory under both Florida law and federal law.[26] Justice Breyer explained that neither the Florida Supreme Court nor the Florida Legislature adopted December 12 as the drop-dead date for counting votes, and that several provisions of federal law obligated Congress to count a State's electoral votes based on election results determined after December 12.[27] Justice Souter wrote: "There is no justification for denying the State the opportunity to try to count all disputed ballots now."[28] (I note that the Court's vote did not divide strictly on party lines. While Justice Breyer and I were appointed by President Clinton, a Democrat, our colleagues in dissent were appointed by Republican presidents: Justice Stevens by President Ford, Justice Souter by President Bush, the elder.)

Less than two months into the aftermath, I will not venture any dire or definitive declarations about the implications of *Bush v. Gore* for judicial independence. The wisdom of the Court's decision to intervene, and the wisdom of its ultimate determination, as I said earlier, await history's judgment. The initial commentary has been mixed. *Washington Post* columnist Robert Novak, fearing a tumultuous political climax in the United States Congress had the recounts gone forward, praised "the bare majority of the high court" for "sav[ing] the country from th[e] potential constitutional crisis

resulting from Gore's doggedness."[29] Columnist Charles Krauthammer agreed: "Political tension would only have grown—this would
not have been resolved until January!—and created a train wreck.
The majority of the court wisely declined this reckless invitation to a
true constitutional crisis."[30]

On the other side, author and columnist E. J. Dionne wrote: "The
most troublesome aspect here is *not* that the five most conservative
appointees on the court ruled in favor of the Republican presidential
candidate. It is that the same five chose to intrude in Florida's election process having always claimed to be champions of the rights of
states and foes of 'judicial activism' and 'judicial overreach.'"[31] Five
hundred fifty-four law professors signed on to a full-page newspaper
ad declaiming in boldface: "It is Not the Job of a Federal Court to
Stop Votes From Being Counted."[32] And the *New York Times*
reporter whose beat is the U.S. Supreme Court, Linda Greenhouse,
observed: "[T]hese are justices who are accustomed to both bitter
division—often by the same 5-to-4 alignment—and to moving on to
the next case. But there is something different about *Bush v. Gore*
that raises the question about whether moving on will be quite so
easy. This was something more than a dispute rooted in judicial philosophy. . . . [H]ad members of the majority been true to their judicial philosophy, the opinion would have come out differently."[33]

Additional analysis, commentary, even counting are in the works,
and I shall leave the flowing streams of words saved on p.c.'s to the
books and articles certain to appear. It may be fitting, however, to
close my account of *Bush v. Gore* with this parting observation. In
the weeks before the Court decided to hear the case, the editorial
pages of major newspapers (though far from unanimous) contained
abundant commentary urging the Court to end the election controversy with a swift and final resolution. A national crisis was loom-
ing, this commentary maintained, and only the Supreme Court
could avert it. The popular conservative columnist William Safire,
an unlikely proponent of judicial intervention, wrote: "The Supreme
Court (whose unanimous ruling against Nixon on the tapes led to
his resignation) [can] put its imprimatur on the best way to decide
who shall occupy the presidency. And the vast majority of Americans would readily accept the decision."[34] Less acceptable, perhaps,
was the judicial solution proposed in a cartoon handed to me at a
reception. It said: "I think they should let Ruth Bader Ginsburg flip
a coin."

Coin-flipping aside, these sentiments reflect, it seems to me, long
and widely held trust in the fairness and reasoned decision making
of the U.S. federal judiciary. That trust is attributable not only to
the fact that the United States Constitution, for well over 200 years,

has been understood to arm federal courts with authority defini-
tively to declare the law, even in turbulent controversies involving
the Nation's fundamental law. It is also a product of decision making mores to which legions of federal judges adhere: restraint, economy, prudence, respect for other agencies of decision (an element
elaborated on by Professor Dyzenhaus in his lecture),[35] reasoned
judgment, and, above all, fidelity to law. Whatever final judgment
awaits *Bush v. Gore* in the annals of history, I am certain that the
good work and good faith of the U.S. federal judiciary as a whole will
continue to sustain public confidence at a level never beyond repair.

II.

From reading or listening to what some members of the U.S. Congress and the press say about the courts, I acknowledge, one might
not grasp the reality that, almost invariably, federal judges
endeavor to administer justice impartially and to interpret the law
reasonably and sensibly, with due restraint and fidelity to precedent. In some political circles, it has become fashionable to criticize
and even threaten federal judges who decide cases without regard to
what the "home crowd" wants.

One powerful member of the U.S. Congress, Tom DeLay, has advo-
cated the impeachment of judges who render unpopular decisions
that, in his view, do not follow the law. Mr. DeLay, who is not a lawyer but, I'm told, an exterminator by profession,[36] placed on his list
of judicial pests a district court judge in San Antonio, Texas, who
held up certification of the election of two Republican victors in
races for county sheriff and county commissioner. The judge had
issued a stay pending state court resolution of a charge that absentee ballots were counted from persons whose only tie to the election
district had been temporary residence on a military base located in
the district.[37] Once the state court held the ballots valid, the federal
judge promptly vacated the stay order.[38] In justification of his effort
to expand the use of impeachment, Congressman DeLay commented
that federal judges "need to be intimidated."[39]

If Mr. DeLay's initiative should come to pass, then I suppose I
might someday end up on his list of impeachment targets—perhaps
even for reasons beyond my control. In October 1996, for example,
the Associated Press misreported a talk I gave at Louisiana State
University. The report said that I called the United States Constitution outdated and "very skimpy on individual rights."[40] In fact,
while recognizing that human rights charters composed by the U.N.

and by other nations after World War II are more fully framed, I praised the U.S. Constitution as it has evolved over the course of the Nation's history.[41]

Although the AP printed a correction,[42] bad news, however distorted or incorrect, is not easily erased. A sampling of letters received in chambers from readers of the incorrect release: I deplore your "alien, Anti-American ideology." "I am ashamed that you were ever appointed to your position and especially ashamed that you are a woman." "Your extreme views are outrageous. I am calling for your resignation."

Unnerving as such threats may be, I think the *New York Times* columnist Bob Herbert got it right when he said in a December 2000 column, "An intimidated judge is a worthless judge."[43] There are

---

Recent congressional attacks on judicial independence have included what can fairly be described as political hazing of federal judicial nominees.

---

good reasons why the United States Constitution guarantees that federal judges "shall hold their Offices during good Behaviour,"[44] and the U.S. Congress, for the most part comprehending those reasons, has historically given the term "good Behaviour" a broad construction.

In the 211 years since the ratification of the U.S. Constitution, the House of Representatives has impeached only eleven federal judges; in only five instances did impeachment result in a Senate conviction;[45] and those judges were impeached not for wrongly interpreting the law, but for committing such grave crimes as bribery, racketeering, tax evasion, and perjury.[46] Impeachment is an extraordinary measure, and nothing in current judicial behavior warrants a departure from the historical norm. With all due respect to critics like Mr. DeLay, casual use of impeachment would disserve not only the federal judiciary but also the constitutional principles that have seen the United States through its worst crises.

In addition to threats of impeachment, recent congressional attacks on judicial independence have included what can fairly be described as political hazing of federal judicial nominees. The confirmation process too often strays from examining the qualifications of each nominee into an endeavor to uncover some hidden agenda the nominee supposedly has. In the words of Abner J. Mikva, my former colleague and once chief judge of the United States Court of Appeals for the D.C. Circuit, some of the reasons for congressional inaction in the confirmation process "are too trivial to be real."[47]

One senator blocked the nomination of a Texas state court judge for a federal trial court judgeship in part because of the candidate's conscientious objector status during the Vietnam War. The expressed concern was that he might be biased in cases involving defense contractors.[48] A nominee in California, senior partner in a large law firm, was asked how she voted on over 100 California referenda in recent years.[49] She attracted senators' suspicion for a speech she delivered while president of the California Bar Association. The speech stirring opposition described the difficulties women lawyers face when trying to meld careers and parenthood, and suggested that law firms, in their own self interest, take a fresh look at their policies for career advancement.[50] The nominee was eventually confirmed, but only after waiting more than two years.[51]

A brilliant lawyer in Washington, D.C., never even gained the nomination President Clinton contemplated for him because decades ago he wrote an article criticizing the legal treatment of poverty in the United States.[52] A federal trial court judge in North Carolina, nominated for a court of appeals seat, was attacked because, sitting by designation, he served on an appellate panel that issued a per curiam decision overturning a conviction due to a juror's misconduct.[53] That nomination languished in the Senate for three years and ultimately died in 1998 without a hearing.[54]

Intruding politics prominently into the confirmation process has meant long delays in filling judicial vacancies, and delay, in the face of mounting caseloads, has threatened to erode the quality of justice the U.S. federal judiciary can provide. The trend is unsettling. "During his first six years in office, President Clinton took an average of 75 more days to nominate a candidate for the federal judiciary than President Carter took."[55] "During the 105th Congress of 1997-98, the Senate took an average of 163 more days to act on a nomination (or let it expire) than the Senate did in the 95th Congress of 1977-78."[56]

Last March, the Senate confirmed two nominees for the Ninth Circuit Court of Appeals. One had waited two years for a vote; the other had waited over four years (1,506 days to be exact), the longest wait for any judicial nominee in United States history. While praising these overdue confirmations, Senator Leahy of Vermont, a member of the Judiciary Committee, warned that delaying tactics "risk tearing down the independence of our federal judiciary."[57]

At the end of the year 2000, 43 of the 665 authorized federal trial court seats were vacant, as were 26 of the 179 seats authorized for federal appellate bench judgeships. It remains to be seen how President Bush, facing a Senate evenly divided between Republicans and Democrats, will fare with his judicial nominees.[58] Yet whatever the party division in Congress, the performance of the federal judiciary depends critically, as I see it, on efforts to streamline the nomination and confirmation process. As an independent panel of scholars, former judges, and attorneys appointed by the University of Virginia has concluded, the largest problem in the federal judiciary—the mounting caseload—could be tackled far more effectively if vacancies were filled expeditiously.[59]

Recent efforts to limit judicial independence have also included initiatives more systematic than impeachment threats or confirmation politics. In 1998, the House of Representatives passed a measure called the Judicial Reform Act.[60] Among other things, the bill would have allowed civil litigants to get a case reassigned to another judge simply by objecting to the judge to whom it was originally assigned. Although the bill died in the Senate, it prompted a *New York Times* editorial writer to comment that "[t]he nation has more to fear from Congressional assaults on the traditional powers and independence of the Federal judiciary than from the imagined legion of 'activist' judges that right-wing politicians rant about."[61]

Even worse for the U.S. federal system, in my view, is a proposal, once advanced by my former D.C. Circuit colleague Robert H. Bork, aimed at increasing popular control. His suggestion was to amend the Constitution to authorize Congress, by a majority vote of each House, to overrule any federal or state court decision resolving a constitutional question.[62] Canada, Judge Bork recently noted, had adopted such a measure;[63] its "ineffectiveness" there, Bork said, "caused [him] to abandon [his] own proposal."[64] (Professor Dyzenhaus, if I correctly grasp his paper, holds a different view. He referred positively to the Canadian experiment and appears to find democratic merit in legislative overrides of this order.[65]) A Canadian colleague informed me in November of a less modest proposal. The leading opposition party in Canada lately proposed that decisions of that country's Supreme Court "be referred to Parliament for approval before taking effect to ensure they reflect the 'will of the people' personified in the elected Members of Parliament."[66]

A constitution providing for legislative preview or review of court decisions resolving constitutional questions, the author and journalist Anthony Lewis observed, "would be more democratic in the sense that it would remove constraints on majority rule."[67] But Lewis rightly reminds us, in the words of Aharon Barak, president of the Supreme Court of Israel: "'Democracy is not only majority rule. Democracy is also the rule of basic values . . . values upon which the whole democratic structure is built, and which even the majority cannot touch.'"[68]

The founders of the United States never envisioned a rule of law based on pure majoritarianism,[69] and I see no cause to embark on such an experiment now. As Chief Justice Rehnquist has observed:

> The framers of the United States Constitution came up with two quite original ideas—the first[,] . . . a chief executive who [is] not responsible to the legislature, as a Chief Executive is under the parliamentary system. The second[,] . . . the idea of an independent judiciary with the authority to declare laws passed by Congress unconstitutional. The first idea . . . has not been widely copied by other nations. . . . But the second idea, that of an independent judiciary with the final authority to interpret a written constitution, has caught on [abroad], particularly since the end of the Second World War. It is one of the crown jewels of our system of government today.[70]

I am hopeful that the jewel will remain bright despite the December storm over the U.S. Supreme Court.

III.

To some extent, I think, assaults on judges from the political branches stem from a certain jealousy (federal judges have life tenure and face no periodic election campaigns[71]) or misperception about activities in which judges engage or should engage. Activities like this visit to the University of Melbourne Law School, for example, were the subject of a Senate inquiry not long ago. Senator Grassley of Iowa, chairman of the Senate Judiciary Committee's Subcommittee on Administrative Oversight and the Courts, sent a survey to federal appellate and trial court judges in 1996 inquiring about extracurricular activities. Questions included:

a) Are you involved in . . . teaching, lecturing, writing law review articles . . . ?

b) If so, how much time do you spend on these activities, including preparation and travel?

c) [W]hat is the compensation you receive for such activities?[72]

Many judges found the survey disquieting. Some—like Ralph Winter, then chief judge of the United States Court of Appeals for the Second Circuit and a former Yale Law School teacher—found it a good chance to educate, "an opportunity to dispel myths."[73]

An overwhelming majority of the appellate judges who responded to the survey (and a large majority did respond) reported: Yes, indeed, they are involved in extracurricular educational and professional activities—notably teaching, lecturing, and occasionally writing law review articles.[74] Almost all performed such undertakings without personal compensation, accepting only travel expense coverage. Responding to the Senate survey, the Executive Committee of the United States Judicial Conference explained that "[f]ederal judges have a long and distinguished history of service to the legal profession through their writing, speaking, and teaching,"[75] and emphasized that interaction between law schools, bar associations, and judges should be encouraged, not viewed with suspicion.

> *Happily, I am able to report that lawyers are not remaining silent in the face of irresponsible criticism of judges.*

Senator Grassley published the final results of his study in March 1998.[76] In a press release accompanying the study, the senator remarked that many trips made by judges "were to exotic locations and for purposes which appear far removed from judicial work."[77] He singled out for criticism a federal trial court judge sitting in California, John Davies, who traveled to Australia in April 1996 to attend a conference sponsored by the Australian Swim Coaches Association. Closer inspection of the alleged junket reveals a different story. According to the *Legal Times*, Judge Davies, an Australian native and a 1952 gold medal Olympic swimmer, was flown to Australia by his former swim club to speak at an event and used the trip to visit his terminally ill mother. Davies pointed out that he had not missed a single day of work in 1996 prior to his trip.[78]

In any event, much of the travel logged by U.S. federal judges is not for personal reasons, but for congressionally mandated administrative duties, for judicial education and training, or for informing judges from other countries about our legal system, and learning about the approach of other nations to common problems. I think even Senator Grassley would agree that such travel is legitimate, notwithstanding his exhortation that federal judges "stay home and mind the store."[79]

IV.

Happily, I am able to report that lawyers are not remaining silent in the face of irresponsible criticism of judges. Bar associations—state, local, and national—have helped the public to understand that both restraint and courage are qualities the good jurist must have, and that independence is essential to the preservation of courage. The public, it seems, is receptive to the message. In a 1996 poll, 84 percent of responders agreed it was unreasonable for a President or member of Congress to try to influence a federal judge's decision in a pending case. And 83 percent thought it inappropriate to use judicial decisions as targets in political campaigns.[80]

I confess that, in my views on the prime place of independence for U.S. federal judges, I am an "originalist." I am mindful of one of the grievances against King George III enumerated in the United States Declaration of Independence: "He [the King] has made judges dependent on his Will alone, for the Tenure of their Offices, and the Amount and Payment of their Salaries."[81] I side with James Madison, and will recall his words when he introduced in Congress the amendments that became the United States Constitution's Bill of Rights:

> [I]ndependent tribunals of justice will consider themselves in a peculiar manner the guardians of th[e]se rights; they will be an impenetrable bulwark against every assumption of power in the Legislative or Executive; they will be naturally led to resist every encroachment upon rights expressly stipulated for in the Constitution by the declaration of rights.[82]

Echoing Madison 150 years later, Justice Hugo Black said that it is the authority and responsibility of the Third Branch to "stand against any winds that blow as havens of refuge for those who might otherwise suffer because they are helpless, weak, outnumbered, or because they are non-conforming victims of prejudice and public excitement."[83]

May Madison's vision remain a beacon. And may I close with the words of two U.S. legal scholars from different ends of the political spectrum—one, Bruce Fein, known for his "conservative perspective," the other, Burt Neuborne, known for his "progressive vision." Though often on opposite sides in debate, they recently joined together to speak with one voice on the value of judicial independence. Their co-authored essay[84] concludes:

> Judicial independence in the United States strengthens ordered liberty, domestic tranquility, the rule of law, and democratic ideals. At least in our political culture, it has proved superior to any alternative form of discharging the judicial function that

has ever been tried or conceived. It would be folly to squander this priceless constitutional gift to placate the clamors of benighted political partisans.[85]

Notes:

1. Ruth Bader Ginsburg, "Judicial Independence," 72 *Australian L.J.* 611 (August 1998); Ruth Bader Ginsburg, "Remarks on Judicial Independence," 20 *U. Haw. L. Rev.* 603 (Winter 1998).

2. *See, e.g.*, Stephen Fidler, "U.S. Election: The Final Chapter," *Financial Times*, Dec. 14, 2000, at 14; Stephen Collinson, "Al Gore Weighs Conceding Defeat after Supreme Court Ruling," *Agence France Presse*, Dec. 13, 2000; "Supreme Victory: Recount Unlikely After Court Decision," *Edmonton Sun*, Dec. 13, 2000; "Gore to Pull Out of White House Race," *Statesman*, Dec. 13, 2000 (India); Roy Eccleston, "Judges' Verdict: It's Bush," *Australian*, Dec. 14, 2000; "Bush Next U.S. President: High Court Reverses Recount Order," *Manila Times*, Dec. 14, 2000; "U.S. Supreme Court Rules for Bush, Gore Urged to Concede," *People's Daily*, Dec. 13, 2000 (China); "U.S. Elections Decided on Strength of One Conservative Judge's Vote," *Tel Aviv Yedi'ot Aharonot*, Dec. 14, 2000, at 2.

3. See William H. Rehnquist, "Dedicatory Address: Act Well Your Part: Therein All Honor Lies," 7 *Pepperdine L. Rev.* 227, 229–30 (1980).

4. Henry Fielding, *Joseph Andrews* 39 (R.F. Brissenden ed., Penguin Books 1977) (1742).

5. 418 U.S. 683 (1974).

6. "Justice Burger's Contradictions," *N.Y. Times*, June 27, 1995, at A16 (editorial).

7. *See, e.g.*, 2 Stephen E. Ambrose, *Nixon: The Triumph of a Politician, 1962–1972*, at 376 (1989).

8. 343 U.S. 579 (1952).

9. *Id.* at 590–91 (appendix to opinion of the Court) (quoting Exec. Order 10340).

10. *Id.* at 589.

11. *Id.* at 666–67 (Clark, J., concurring) (quoting *The Orono*, 18 Fed. Cas. No. 10,585 (Cir. Ct. D. Mass. 1812)).

12. Michael R. Belknap, "Constitutional Law As Creative Problem Solving: Could the Warren Court Have Ended the Vietnam War?," 36 *Cal. W. L. Rev.* 99, 123 (1999) (quoting Stanley I. Kutler, *The Wars of Watergate: The Last Crisis of Richard Nixon* 515 (1990)).

13. 1 Alexis De Tocqueville, *Democracy in America* 280 (Henry Reeve trans., Phillips Bradley ed., Vintage Classics 1990) (1835).

14. 121 S. Ct. 525 (2000).

15. *Bush v. Palm Beach County Canvassing Bd.*, 121 S. Ct. 471 (2000).

16. *Id.* at 474–75 (citing *Minnesota v. National Tea Co.*, 309 U.S. 551, 555 (1940)).

17. 121 U.S. 512 (2000).

18. *Id.* at 512–13 (Stevens, J., joined by Souter, Ginsburg, and Breyer, JJ., dissenting).

19. *Id.* at 512 (Scalia, J., concurring).

20. *Id.* at 512 (Scalia J., concurring) ("The counting of votes that are of questionable legality does in my view threaten irreparable harm to petitioner, and to the country, by casting a cloud upon what he claims to be the legitimacy of his election."); *id.* at 513 (Stevens, J., dissenting) ("Preventing the recount from being completed will inevitably cast a cloud on the legitimacy of the election.").

21. *Bush*, 121 S. Ct. at 530–31.

22. *Id.* at 533.

23. *Id.*

24. *Id.* at 545–46 (Souter, J., dissenting); *id.* at 551 (Breyer, J., dissenting).

25. *Id.* at 540–41 (Stevens, J., dissenting); *id.* at 550 (Ginsburg, J., dissenting).

26. *Id.* at 542 (Stevens, J., dissenting); *id.* at 543, 545 (Souter, J., dissenting); *id.* at 550 (Ginsburg, J., dissenting); *id.* at 556 (Breyer, J., dissenting).

27. *Id.* at 552–53, 556 (Breyer, J., dissenting).

28. *Id.* at 546 (Souter, J., dissenting).

29. Robert D. Novak, "When to Say When," *Wash. Post*, Dec. 14, 2000, at A35.

30. Charles Krauthammer, "Defenders of the Law," *Wash. Post*, Dec. 15, 2000, at A41.

31. E. J. Dionne, Jr., "So Much for States' Rights," *Wash. Post*, Dec. 14, 2000, at A35.

32. "554 Law Professors Say . . . ," *N.Y. Times*, Jan. 13, 2000, at A7.

33. Linda Greenhouse, "Another Kind of Bitter Split," *N.Y. Times*, Dec. 14, 2000, at A1.

34. Williams Safire, "Fight to the Finish," *N.Y. Times*, Nov. 16, 2000, at A35.

35. David Dyzenhaus, "The Justice of the Common Law: Judges, Democracy and the Limits of the Rule of Law" 18 (Nov. 8, 2000).

36. Abner J. Mikva, "The Judges v. the People: Judicial Independence and Democratic Ideals," 52 *Rec. of Ass'n of Bar of City of N.Y.* 791, 793 (1997).

37. *Casarez v. Val Verde County*, 957 F. Supp. 847 (W.D. Tex. 1997).

38. *Casarez v. Val Verde County*, 967 F. Supp. 917 (W.D. Tex. 1997).

39. Joan Biskupic, "Hill Republicans Target 'Judicial Activism'; Conservatives Block Nominees, Threaten Impeachment and Term Limits," *Wash. Post*, Sept. 14, 1997, at A1; *see* Herman Schwartz, "One Man's Activist: What Republicans Really Mean When They Condemn Judicial Activism," *Wash. Monthly*, Nov. 1997, at 10. The recent election controversy has generated backlash of this sort in Florida. *See* Dexter Filkins, "Republican Group Seeks to Unseat Three Justices," *N.Y. Times*, Dec. 20, 2000, at A17.

40. *See, e.g.*, Peter Shinkle, "Justice Ginsburg: Constitution 'Skimpy,'" *Baton Rouge Advocate*, Oct. 25, 1996, at 1B–2B.

41. *See generally* Ruth Bader Ginsburg, "An Overview of Court Review for Constitutionality in the United States," 57 *La. L. Rev.* 1019 (1997).

42. The AP correction circulated on November 4, 1996.

43. Bob Herbert, "A Plan to Intimidate Judges," *N.Y. Times*, Dec. 4, 2000, at A29.

44. *U.S. Const.* art. III, § 1, cl. 2.

45. "Impeaching Federal Judges: Where Are We and Where Are We Going?," 72 *Judicature* 359, 359 (1989).

46. Maria Simon, Note, "Bribery and Other Not So 'Good Behavior': Criminal Prosecution As a Supplement to Impeachment of Federal Judges," 94 *Colum. L. Rev.* 1617, 1617 n. 2 (1994).

47. Mikva, *supra* note 36, at 794.

48. *See* Ron Hutcheson, "Gramm Official Lambastes Nominee," *Fort Worth Star-Telegram*, Nov. 17, 1997, at 1.

49. *See* Viveca Novack, "Empty-Bench Syndrome: Congressional Republicans Are Determined to Put Clinton's Judicial Nominees on Hold," *Time*, May 26, 1997, at 37.

50. *See* Margaret Morrow, Address at the California State Bar Women in the Law Conference (Apr. 30, 1994); *see also* Monica Bay, "Women Urged to Change Profession's Priorities," *Am. Lawyer*, May 9, 1994, at 3.

51. *See* Robert Schmidt, "Federal Judgeships on the Move?," *Recorder*, Feb. 12, 1998, at 1; *see also Uncertain Justice* (Reports of the Task Forces of Citizens for Independent Courts) 24 (The Constitution Project 2000) (reporting that average number of days between nomination and final action for women is greater than the number of days for men).

52. Mikva, *supra* note 36, at 794.

53. *See* Bruce D. Brown, "From the Freying Pan . . . ," *Legal Times*, Apr. 8, 1996, at 6.

54. *See* Betty Winston Baye, "The All-White 4th Circuit: Clinton's Shame," *Courier-Journal*, Mar. 23, 2000, at 13a; "Unpacking the Court," *N.Y. Times*, June 13, 1998, at A20 (editorial); Hermann Schwartz, "Playing Racial Politics with Judgeships," *Newsday*, Feb. 26, 1998, at A41.

55. *Uncertain Justice, supra* note 51, at 21. Average days for presidential action were 240 for Carter, 315 for Clinton. *See id.* at 40.

56. *Id.* at 21. Average days for Senate action were 38 in the 1977-78 Congress, 201 in the 1997-1998 Congress. *See id.* at 40.

57. Harriet Chiang & Carolyn Lochhead, "2 Confirmed to Court in S.F. After Long Battle in Senate," *S.F. Chron.*, Mar. 10, 2000, at A1.

58. *See* Linda Greenhouse, "The Legal Spectacle; Divining the Consequences of a Court Divided," *N.Y. Times*, Dec. 17, 2000, sec. 4, at 1 ("The chance that a nominee as ideologically combative as Justice Scalia, whose confirmation vote 13 years ago was 98-0, would be confirmed today, at least without a major battle in a closely divided Senate, appears almost impossible.").

59. *See* Jonathan Groner, "Grassley's Poll," *Legal Times*, May 20, 1996, at 6.

60. *See* H. R. 1252, 105th Cong. (1998).

61. "Tampering with the Judiciary," *N.Y. Times*, Apr. 23, 1998, at A24 (editorial).

62. *See* Robert H. Bork, "Slouching towards Gomorrah" 117 (1996).

63. *See* Canadian Charter of Rights and Freedoms art. 33 (permitting the national Parliament and provincial legislatures to declare an act or provision operative notwithstanding conflict with rights prescribed in the Charter). A legislative override of a prescribed right sunsets after five years, but may be reenacted for another five-year period. *Id.*
64. Robert H. Bork, "Rein on Judges: A Long Tradition," Dec. 12, 2000, at A23 (letter to the editor).
65. Dyzenhaus, *supra* note 35, at 24–25, 28.
66. Letter to Justice Ruth Bader Ginsburg from Ed Ratushny, Q.C., Professor of Law, University of Ottawa (November 16, 2000).
67. Anthony Lewis, "Why the Courts," *Record*, Mar./Apr. 2000, at 178, 181.
68. *Id.* (quoting Aharon Barak, president of the Supreme Court of Israel).
69. *See* U.S. Const. art. III; *The Federalist* No. 51 (James Madison).
70. William H. Rehnquist, "Keynote Address at the Washington College of Law Centennial Celebration" (Apr. 9, 1996), *in* Symposium on the Future of the Federal Courts, 46 *Am. U. L. Rev.* 263, 273–74 (1996).
71. *U.S. Const.* art. III, § 1. I do not address in these remarks the very different situation in 42 of the 50 States in which, according to the American Bar Association, at least some judges face elections. *See* William Glaberson, "Chief Justices to Meet on Abuses in Judicial Races," *N.Y. Times*, Sept. 8, 2000, at A14; *see also Uncertain Justice, supra* note 51, at 89 (Currently, "77 percent of all judges on [trial] courts of general jurisdiction and 53 percent of all appellate court judges in the states face contestable elections.").
72. *Staff of Senate Subcomm. On Admin. Oversight and the Courts of the Senate Comm. On the Judiciary, 104th Cong., Report on the Jan. 1996 Judicial Survey*, pt. 2, app. A, at 2 (1996) [hereinafter Senate Report].
73. Deborah Pines & Bill Alden, "District, Circuit Judges Use Senate Survey to Boast, Gripe," *N.Y.L.J.*, Mar. 25, 1996, at 1.
74. *See Senate Report, supra* note 72, at 49.
75. *Response of the Exec. Comm. of the Judicial Conf. of the United States to the Judicial Survey*, Feb. 26, 1996, at 19.
76. *See U.S. General Accounting Office, Federal Judiciary: Information on Noncase-Related Travel of Article III Judges in 6 Circuits and 34 Districts* (1998).
77. Robert Schmidt, "Federal Judges in the Jet Set," *Legal Times*, Apr. 6, 1998, at 6.
78. *Id.*
79. *Id.*
80. John Gibeaut, "Taking AIM," 82 *A.B.A.J.* 50, 52 (1996).
81. *The Declaration of Independence* para. 11 (U.S. 1776).
82. James Madison, Address to the House of Representatives (June 8, 1789), reprinted in *The Mind of the Founder* 224 (Marvin Meyers ed., 1973).
83. *Chambers v. Florida*, 309 U.S. 227, 241 (1940).
84. Bruce Fein & Burt Neuborne, "Why Should We Care about Independent and Accountable Judges?," 84 *Judicature* 58 (2000).
85. *Id.* at 64.

The Recent Presidential Election

The Residual Effects on the Courts[2]

Mary J. Mullarkey

Chief Justice, Colorado Supreme Court, 1998– ; born New London, WI, September 28, 1943; B.A., cum laude graduate in mathematics, St. Norbert College, WI, 1965; LL.B., Harvard Law School, 1968; attorney-advisor, Water and Power Resources Division (1968–70) and Civil Rights Branch (1970–73), Department of Interior; Assistant Regional Attorney, EEOC, 1973–75; First Assistant Attorney General—Appellate, 1975–79; Solicitor General, Colorado Department of Law, 1979–82; legal advisor to Colorado Governor Richard D. Lamm, 1982–85; partner, Mullarkey and Seymour, 1985–87; Associate Justice, Colorado Supreme Court, 1987–93; member, Colorado Bar, Denver Bar, Colorado Women's Bar, American Bar Association, and Conference of Chief Justices; Colorado Bar Foundation Fellow and American Bar Foundation Fellow; St. Norbert College Alumni Award for Distinguished Achievement in the Humanities, 1980; honorary Doctor of Laws, St. Norbert College, 1989; Colorado Women's Bar Association Recognition Award, 1986.

Editors' introduction: Chief Justice Mary J. Mullarkey spoke to 75 members and guests of The Denver Forum, a longtime association of businesses and individuals interested in the issues facing Colorado and the Nation. This address, in the Oxford Hotel Banquest Room, downtown Denver, was one in an ongoing series of speeches by community and national leaders on current issues. Concerned that "public confidence in the courts will suffer" because of "recent presidential election cases," Chief Justice Mary J. Mullarkey addressed "the purpose and role of courts in America," asserting that "the voting system" should be "fixed before the next election."

Mary J. Mullarkey's speech: Perhaps you saw, as I did, an article last week in the Denver *Rocky Mountain News* reporting on an opinion poll conducted in Colorado about the 2000 presidential election. According to the article, 57% of the respondents thought that the United States Supreme Court reached the right result when it stopped the hand counting of Florida ballots. Thirty-seven percent thought the hand counting should have been completed. Another

---

2. Delivered in Denver, Colorado, on January 16, 2001, at a noon luncheon. Reprinted with permission of Mary J. Mullarkey.

question asked was "Do you think the recent U.S. Supreme Court decision on the election created greater or lesser confidence in the judicial system by the general public?" Forty-nine percent replied that the decision created less confidence, 30% said there was no difference and 15% thought the decision caused the public to have greater confidence in the courts.

What's going on here? How can a sizable majority of Coloradans think that the court reached the right result and at the same time, most of those people think that the court's decision undermined public trust and confidence in the judiciary? Were the poll respondents merely confused? Are the poll results consistent?

The answer, I think, belongs in understanding the purpose and role of courts in America. The goal of our justice system is stated very clearly in the motto engraved above the entrance to the U.S. Supreme Court building. That inscription reads: "Equal Justice Under Law."

As I understand it, when that inscription was chosen, there was some debate about the inclusion of the word "equal" in the saying. After all, the argument went, isn't the concept of equal treatment inherent in the meaning of justice? Is it ever possible to have true justice without equality under the law?

We know that courts are supposed to be the great levelers in our society. A court is the one place where disputes are supposed to be decided on the merits. It is to be a forum where unequal power, wealth, or prestige and other similar characteristics that divide the parties are irrelevant. The case is decided by a dispassionate, objective judge, who understands his or her own biases and is able to set them aside. Equal justice demands decision makers who are courageous, who are able "to do the right thing" while knowing full well that the results may be controversial and the fallout for the decision-makers may be unfair criticisms.

Those are tall orders for the mere mortals who are judges. To the extent that our court system has been able to live up to these lofty goals, it has been because of the process employed by the courts.

The results of the *Rocky Mountain News* poll seem consistent with the research. Social scientists have tried to identify why people follow or obey court decisions even when they do not agree with the results reached in the decision. The courts have no armies to enforce their decisions. They have no funds to pay damages. If you think about it, Americans' commitment to the rule of law is quite remarkable.

It is often noted that courts have no real ability to enforce their decisions. True, the courts can hold people in contempt and jail or fine them. But judges do not execute those orders. For the most part, we as a society accept and obey court decisions even when the decision may cost one's life, liberty or fortune. Think for a moment about President Eisenhower using troops to enforce the school desegregation decisions even though he himself may not have agreed with the decisions or the timing of the decisions.

The Supreme Court's role as the final interpreter of the constitution developed during the long tenure of John Marshall as chief justice. In his separate dissenting opinion in *Bush v. Gore*, Justice Breyer refers to President Andrew Jackson's purported response to a Supreme Court decision holding unconstitutional Georgia's Indian laws. "John Marshall has made his decision; now let him enforce it."

Jackson probably never made that remark, although Jacksonian Democrats attacked the independence of the judiciary. Jackson strongly asserted federal supremacy. Much to Marshall's delight,

---

Studies have shown that, for most people, the process used by a court in making its decision is actually more important than the result reached.

Jackson said the Supreme Court was the ultimate arbiter of the meaning of the constitution and if the court upheld the constitutionality of a statute, its order must be obeyed. Justice Breyer's point, however, is correct. Supreme Court decisions have been greeted with defiance as well as acceptance. Another image from the school desegregation days is that of Alabama Governor George Wallace standing in the school house door to block integration.

There are two strong themes at play here that help explain why people follow court decisions. The first, according to the research of social scientists, is attributable to the fairness of the court process. The studies have shown that, for most people, the process used by a court in making its decision is actually more important than the result reached. A party can lose a case but accept the result if the court is perceived as being fair. Conversely, winning a case may leave the victor angry and embittered if the process is seen as unfair. Americans greatly value the opportunity to be heard and treated respectfully by the decision-maker.

The second factor explaining public acceptance of judicial decisions is the credibility that courts have accumulated over a long period of time. Certainly institutional concerns that the actions of the majority threatened the objectivity of the court seemed to motivate the dissenters in both the Florida Supreme Court and the U.S. Supreme Court.

Let's look at how those factors played themselves out in the recent presidential election. Was the court process fair and perceived as being fair? Here, I think we run up against some of the inherent limitations of the appellate decision-making process. Although we who sit on appellate courts cannot take forever to decide cases, we have the luxury of relatively much time to make our decisions. The process is very formal and predictable. There are occasional emergencies but they don't happen often and usually can be avoided.

This case presented an emergency of the highest order, one that could not be postponed. One of the separate opinions in *Bush v. Gore* tells us that the Florida Supreme Court issued each of its two opinions within 29 hours of hearing the oral arguments. Clearly, the justices acted very quickly. They had very little time to absorb the parties' arguments, do their own research and make their decision. There was almost no time for reflection, dialog or give-and-take among the justices. For the most part, they must have had to rely on their initial impressions and go with that. The same was also true for the Supreme Court. Although it did not turn around the case quite as fast as the Florida Supreme Court, it acted with lightning speed compared to its usual time table.

This abrupt departure from their normal way of doing things must have placed enormous pressures on the justices of both courts. In my experience with high profile, controversial cases, my first take on the case is often flawed. It takes time to understand these complex ideas and to work through the possible ramifications of pursuing different courses of action. Taking the time to consider my colleagues' views doesn't necessarily cause me to change my vote as to the ultimate outcome. But it has caused me to adopt a different and better rationale for the decision. Some of my best opinions have resulted from being confronted by a vigorous dissent that exposed the weaknesses of my reasoning. It's not fun to go through the experience of re-thinking and completely re-writing a draft opinion, but it can be worth doing. When it works, that shows the value of a multi-member court at its best.

Consider, for example, the process that led to the *Brown v. Board of Education* school desegregation decision. The decision is a short, unanimous opinion. It was the result of years of litigation. The case was argued twice in the Supreme Court in two successive years. The Chief Justice worked long and hard to put the full weight of the court behind one opinion. By contrast, neither the Florida Supreme Court nor the United States Supreme Court had time for reflection and study in this case. Brilliant as they may be, I doubt that any of them had thought very deeply about the issues raised by this election before they were confronted by this case.

The speed with which these two courts were forced to act was an abrupt departure from the normal practice. The fact that the Supreme Court chose to insert itself into the process in the first place was also a surprise to most observers. In retrospect one of the most ironic statements was made by the U.S. District Court Judge who refused to intervene in Florida's vote counting approximately one week after election day. He said, "The body of law is pretty pervasive that the federal courts ought to stay out of state elections."

The unusual course followed by the two appellate courts can be explained, but the effect was to undercut the validity of the process. When nearly one-half of the Coloradans surveyed believed that the Supreme Court's decision had diminished public support for the court, I think they were expressing doubts about the fairness of the process. They did not believe the process was fair even though many of them agreed with the result reached by the majority. The process was too hurried and chaotic to inspire confidence. Unlike the short unanimous opinion in *Brown v. Board of Education*, there are multiple opinions in *Bush v. Gore*. Separate views are expressed for 7 of the 9 justices.

Harsh attacks have been launched against both courts. Don't get me wrong. Courts are not above criticism. One of the jobs of an appellate court is to lay out its reasoning in writing as clearly and persuasively as it can. That's not an easy thing to do. I've been on the court long enough to have many of my opinions cited back to me. Sometimes I think to myself: "That's not what I meant." Or "I certainly could have phrased it better."

Much of the criticism directed to the two courts in this case has not been directed to the merits of the decisions but rather has impugned the motives of the various justices. There have been reports of groups targeting certain Florida justices for removal from office.

That's troubling. Not unexpected given the nature of the controversy, but troubling nonetheless. Where is the leadership, whether in or out of government, whether at the state or federal level, to support the rule of law and the independence of the judiciary? When the country is so deeply and evenly divided as it was in this election, it would seem especially important to draw together and support our institutions of government, imperfect as they may be.

Both Justice Thomas and Chief Justice Rehnquist have commented on the accusations that the majority was motivated by partisan politics. Justice Thomas, speaking to high school students, said that the rules of the political world do not apply to the Supreme Court. He added, "I have yet to hear any discussion in nine years of partisan politics among members of the court." The chief justice agreed with Justice Thomas' observations.

Later in his written year-end report to Congress, Rehnquist stated that this presidential election "tested our constitutional system in ways it has never been tested before. The Florida state courts, the lower federal courts and the Supreme Court became involved in a way that one hopes will seldom, if ever, be necessary in the future."

Some analysts have claimed that the Supreme Court has inflicted lasting damage on itself. That remains to be seen. The Supreme Court has survived many cycles of intense criticism in its 200 plus year history. The correctness of the decision and its soundness also remain to be seen. The opinion may have been produced in haste but it will be analyzed and re-analyzed at leisure. No doubt it will be examined in exquisite detail by generations of law professors to come.

When the country is so deeply and evenly divided as it was in this election, it would seem especially important to draw together and support our institutions of government.

Of course, none of us knows how the case will be interpreted. We don't know if, for example, its equal protection analysis can be limited to the facts of this election, as the opinion suggests. No doubt the scope of the decision must be limited if the Supreme Court wants to avoid micromanaging the work of the state supreme courts.

The aftermath of this series of judicial decisions is likely to affect the rest of us who are judges. Highly publicized decisions reflect on all courts whether they are directly involved or not. During the O. J. Simpson trial, respect for all courts seemed to drop as the public became dissatisfied with Judge Ito's widely televised performance. Our state court administrator's office received phone calls from people wishing to complain about Judge Ito. When we tried to explain that he was a California judge and not a Colorado judge, the usual response was: "I don't care. I want to file a complaint anyway."

Similarly, we have benefited from cases that we had nothing to do with. When Judge Matsch was seen by the public as doing a good job in the Oklahoma City bombing trial, we benefited from the good will he generated.

The recent presidential election cases also will have a residual effect on the courts nationwide and right now that effect looks negative. The public saw the judicial process as unfair and, as a result, public confidence in the courts will suffer. The perception of unfairness is caused by inherent limitations of the appellate process and nothing more sinister. Just as Chief Justice Rehnquist expressed his hope that the courts will never again be involved in this type of case, my hope is that the voting system is fixed before the next election so that this kind of case will not happen again.

Cleveland City Club[3]

Thomas J. Moyer

Chief Justice of the Supreme Court of Ohio, 1987– ; born April 18, 1939, Sandusky, OH; B.A., Ohio State University, 1961; J.D., Ohio State University, 1964; Assistant Attorney General, Taxation and Workers' Compensation Sections, 1964–66; private law practice, 1966–69; Probate Court Referee for Commitments to Columbus State Hospital, 1968; Deputy Assistant to Governor, 1969–71; Crabbe, Brown, Jones, Potts, & Schmidt law firm, 1972–75; Executive Assistant to Ohio governor James A. Rhodes, 1975–79; Judge of Tenth District Court of Appeals, 1979–86, Ohio, and Presiding Judge, 1985; president, Columbus Bar Association, 1980–81; Board of Trustees, Franklin University, 1986–87; chairs Board of Directors, Ohio State University Alumni Association, and Criminal Sentencing Commission; former president, National Conference of Chief Justices; co-chairs national committee to develop model legislation for mediation in state courts; Honorary Doctor of Laws from several colleges and universities; public service awards from various private foundations and civic groups.

Editors' introduction: Chief Justice Thomas J. Moyer addressed the Cleveland City Club, the oldest continuous free speech forum in the United States. Since 1912, this nonpartisan club has "encouraged new ideas and a free exchange of thought." In his speech, Judge Moyer assessed recommendations made by the Ohio Courts Futures commission for improving the judiciary. Using an example from the 2000 presidential campaign, the Chief Justice warned that "the integrity of the court and judicial independence are threatened when judges are politically attacked for the manner in which they exercise their judgment."

Thomas J. Moyer's speech: It is an honor to be the first speaker to be invited to the Cleveland City Club in what some regard as the actual new millennium. This is the fourth opportunity I have had to speak—last was in October to assist in the induction of Dick Pogue. One thousand years from now, when museum-keepers examine this period of time, they will not note what I say here, but they will come to the "citadel of free speech" to reflect on the events of the 21st century.

---

3. Delivered in Cleveland, Ohio, on January 5, 2001, at noon. Reprinted with permission of Thomas J. Moyer.

For nearly 90 years, the City Club has been a vibrant demonstration of Jeffersonian democracy: a forum for Roosevelts and Kennedys; Reagan and Rhodes; Hoffa and Ness. The City Club is a vital forum for the competition of ideas.

Jurors should be given a more active role.

As always, at the end of 2000, the media released its lists of greatest leaders, greatest athletes and, of course, it named the "man of the year." They did us a favor. By looking back they cleared the way for us to look forward.

A crucial responsibility of every public and private institution is planning for the future. The judiciary is no exception. The institution is crucial to orderly change in our times. The Ohio Courts Futures Commission developed more than sixty recommendations that mark a path into the first quarter of this century. Last year the Commission's 52 members issued their final report that included topics ranging from changes in jury service to the level of assistance offered unrepresented litigants, to qualifications of judges. Susan Eagan, co-chaired, Dick Pogue, Bill Gasgill and Linda Ammons.

One set of recommendations is on its way to implementation. The Supreme Court Advisory Commission on Technology is developing technology standards directed at improving communication among all courts, reducing costs, increasing efficiency and enhancing access to information for all citizens.

Jury Service

Jurors should be given a more active role. Some Ohio trial courts already allow jurors to take notes and ask questions of witnesses. These are tasks most of us take for granted, but are denied to most jurors. Reforms in states such as New York, California and Arizona indicate that jurors who are more actively engaged in a trial are better able to understand the issues of a case, and produce more informed decisions. These recommendations will be among others to be considered by the Committee to Implement Jury Reform in Ohio.

One of the most perplexing problems identified in the Futures Commission report is how to ensure that all citizens, regardless of income, education or language skills have access to the state courts. Eighty-four percent of the common pleas courts in Ohio report an increase in pro se litigation over the past five years. And 87 percent of the self-representations occur in domestic and family law cases.

We must not turn our back on pro se litigants. They do require patience and use of court resources. But, the rights to procedural and substantive due process are universal. They are not parsed on the basis of income.

Ensuring fairness also was the task of the Racial Fairness Commission, which presented the court with its final report one year ago. The Commission was chaired by Cleveland Municipal Judge Ronald Adrine, and it found a pervasive perception among minorities that they are not treated fairly by the courts, and that court staffs include few racial minorities. The Commission's conclusion stated: "Platitudes about freedom and equality are not enough; indeed they can become excuses for hidden unfairness. Instead of a leap of faith, what is required is a leap of action to make bold changes to the status quo."

To that end, the Commission recommended a wide range of studies and programs, including the statistical reporting of criminal sentencing, the number of minority court personnel, and the recruitment and retention of minority law students. A task force is working to implement the Commission's recommendations and is expected to submit its final report later this year.

Without waiting for the task force report, the Supreme Court has moved forward to address an issue that will require the assistance of the General Assembly. The retention rate of minority law school students is far lower than that of other students. Therefore, the biennial budget the Court has submitted to the General Assembly requests more than $800,000 to initiate a program that would provide an intensive six-week program during the summer preceding a student's first year of law school, and some financial assistance during law school. A similar program is highly successful in Indiana.

The Futures Commission, the Racial Fairness Commission, in fact, other court-sponsored programs such as drug courts and dispute resolution have a common thread: to ensure the fair and effective administration of the rule of law. All such efforts are intended to preserve and, indeed, enhance trust and confidence in our courts.

Most courts are meeting that challenge. But we can do better. In particular, we can do better in the process by which we select some judges. Judicial campaigns have become politicized as never before, complete with multi-million dollar media campaigns.

In California, a Superior Court judge accused her opponent of being soft on cop-killers and child molesters. The judge now faces disciplinary charges.

In the Michigan Supreme Court races, one candidate was accused of being racist, while another was labeled as lenient in sentencing sex offenders.

And in Ohio, several million dollars were spent on races for two seats on the Supreme Court. It was a difficult campaign year. We must never experience another like it.

Ohio experienced a type of advertising in judicial campaigns never before seen. Television and radio ads attacked the two incumbent justices, not for the way in which they administer their dockets or perform their work or for personal misconduct, but for their decisions in important cases.

The integrity of the court and judicial independence are threatened when judges are politically attacked for the manner in which they exercise their judgment. The danger is that judgments will become political.

In Tennessee, for example, there has been long-term fallout after a supreme court justice was defeated in a highly politicized retention election. Some time after the election another Tennessee justice resigned after he found himself pondering the political ramifications of his judicial decisions.

The fallout in Florida may have just begun. Some political leaders in that state have organized a campaign to defeat two Florida justices when they run in the next retention election. The group's web page includes information on how to impeach a judge.

Citizens may disagree with a judicial decision. Dissent is part of the American spirit, but to extract political revenge, to threaten the tenure of a judge over a decision with which some may disagree, places the judge in the same political position as a mayor or a legislator. It suggests that judges owe some members of their community something other than the impartial resolution of disputes.

Remember Adlai Stevenson's definition of democracy is "where it is safe to be unpopular."

For seven years we worked actively with new leaders—Ukraine—to establish an independent judicial system. One of the dramatic differences is citizen's expectation of courts.

- Ukraine—expectation—telephone justice—no impartiality
- U.S.—expectation—duty of courts, judges—impartiality
- To extent that political campaigns change that expectation/the fundamental principles that make judicial crucial to democracy—are threatened.

Many members of the bench and bar have spent years working to reform our judicial election process. Today, by court rules, judicial campaigns have limits on and full disclosure of contributions, a prohibition on judicial candidates using funds raised while holding another political office and a streamlined system to enforce the rules regulating campaign conduct.

We have done as much as any state, and more than most, to place controls on a very imperfect system for selecting judges. I have called on judges, lawyers and other elected leaders to recommit themselves to greater, more lasting reforms.

I have several thoughts. Some relate to action that should be taken immediately, assuming we continue to elect judges in so-called non-partisan elections. First, we should work with legislative leaders to redefine the definition of "advocacy," a possibility suggested in recent federal court opinions. This is necessary if we are to require outside, independent groups to disclose their expenditures and their contributors.

Second, we should explore, to the extent technologically possible, the feasibility of requiring instantaneous reporting of campaign contributions.

I recognize that these proposals would only chip at the edge of the problems confronting judicial campaigns. When we examine all the alternatives, incremental change in the current system may be all we can accomplish. In my opinion, that is not enough. It is time to fundamentally change the way we select appellate judges in Ohio. We do not have the luxury of being timid. The threats are real and damage has been inflicted.

We can reduce the perception that money and politics matter more than merit and performance.

It has been said that: "Putting courts into politics and compelling judges to become politicians, in many jurisdictions has almost destroyed the traditional respect for the bench." That was Roscoe Pound's observation in 1906 when he spoke to the American Bar Association. It was true then; it is true today.

For years, I have supported amending the Ohio Constitution to remove from the open elective process, the judges of our 12 courts of appeals and the justices of the Supreme Court of Ohio. There is no perfect system; there is no system for selecting judges that will guarantee a judge's character and commitment to the principles upon which our democratic justice system is founded. But we can reduce the perception that money and politics matter more than merit and performance.

In the 50 states and the District of Columbia, 30 have successfully adopted an appointive system to select judges. This leaves Ohio in a minority of 21 states that select appellate judges in open elections.

I believe the time is right. It is right not just for lawyers and judges. It is right for all Ohio citizens. At a very basic level they understand that judges should stand apart from common politics— from aggressive fund raising—from attack ads—all of which diminish the perception, if not the reality, of impartiality.

Our next best opportunity to ask voters to adopt true judicial selection reform comes in the general election in November. Any change of this magnitude will require the support of the bar, the bench, the governor, the General Assembly, the political parties and committed civic groups and individuals.

One final observation—In the closing days of 2000, our nation traveled an unmarked path when it took 36 days to conclude presidential ballot counting. At times it seemed to some that the journey would never end. It was a cynic's dream; but it was not a crisis. It was democracy in its unglamorous splendor.

The experience taught us something about our democracy, renewed our belief in and reliance upon our institutions and, most important, revealed the profound strength of the American character. No one could have wanted the uncertainty; no one could have predicted America's patience. No one could wish that the leader of the executive branch, the most important elected position in the world, would be determined by decisions of the judicial branch. In another time and in many other places the doubt we have experienced would have dissipated with the presence of military force or violent rebellion. But in America we live by a different standard; we live by the rule of law; the American spirit says the peaceful process by which a leader is selected supersedes all concern for the identity of the leader.

All of our institutions embody our belief in that principal and our trust in each other. And it is that trust in our institutions that enables us to tolerate the inefficiencies of democracy and accept the decisions of those who serve its institutions.

We extend such tolerance because we see ourselves in the reflections of our institutions. We see our strengths. We see our weaknesses. We see our future; it provides hope and confidence.

Remarks to the National Consortium of Task Forces and Commissions on Racial and Ethnic Bias in the Courts[4]

Bill Lann Lee

Former Assistant Attorney General for Civil Rights, U.S. Department of Justice, 1997–2001; born and raised in New York City; son of Chinese immigrants; magna cum laude graduate, Yale University, 1971; J.D., Columbia University Law School, 1974; assistant counsel, NAACP Legal Defense and educational Fund, New York City, 1974–82; supervising attorney for civil rights litigation, Center for Law in Public Interest, 1983–88; western regional counsel, NAACP Legal Defense and Educational Fund, Los Angeles, 1989–97; adjunct professor of political science, Fordham University; counsel to Asian American Legal Defense and Education Fund.

Editors' introduction: The National Consortium Task Forces and Commissions on Racial and Ethnic Bias in the Courts is composed of groups from all over the United States working to eliminate bias from their state court systems. Assistant Attorney General Bill Lann Lee spoke at a three-day meeting of the National Consortium at the Marriott at Glenpointe. In the speech, Lee noted "efforts that the Department of Justice has undertaken to increase the confidence of communities, particularly the members of the minority communities, in the judicial system."

Bill Lann Lee's speech: I want to thank the Consortium, and particularly Judge McBeth, your moderator, for inviting the Department of Justice to participate in this year's meeting. The important issues you are tackling over these three days relate very closely to the work of the Civil Rights Division. They are also extremely important to the Attorney General personally. If a community has no faith in the fairness and objectivity of those responsible for enforcing and administering the law, that mistrust undermines the very foundation of our system of justice. When the justice system is perceived to be biased, unfair, disrespectful or unrepresentative, people are less willing to trust and confide in police officers, to

---

4. Delivered in Teaneck, New Jersey, on May 12, 2000.

report crimes that come to their attention, to be witnesses at trials, to serve on juries or to submit civil claims for adjudication.

I would like to take this opportunity to discuss some of the efforts that the Department of Justice has undertaken to increase the confidence of communities, particularly the members of the minority communities, in the judicial system: First, I will discuss a number of initiatives that address how law enforcement agencies operate, and second, efforts to increase minority representation in the bar.

I have just come from Los Angeles where I informed city officials that I had authorized the Civil Rights Division to file a lawsuit challenging a pattern or practice of unconstitutional use of force and false arrests. City officials have stated that they wish to talk about an informal resolution.

The public responses to the shooting of Amadou Diallo and the brutal assault on Abner Louima are signs of a breakdown of trust that exists in many areas of the country.

The problem of police misconduct is an old problem in American communities. But there is something else happening now. The public responses to the shooting of Amadou Diallo and the brutal assault on Abner Louima are signs of a breakdown of trust that exists in many areas of the country. We know we have a problem when, as a recent poll shows, two out of three whites say they have a great deal or quite a lot of confidence in the police—but only one out of four African Americans say the same. A recent Gallup poll also indicated that over half of Americans believe that police engage in the practice of racial profiling, and 81% of them disapprove of the practice. This is a real police-community relations problem that everyone can agree needs to be addressed. As the President put it this spring in Selma, Alabama, at the foot of the Edmund Pettus Bridge to commemorate the 35th Anniversary of the Voting Rights Act: "As long as African Americans and Latinos anywhere in America believe they are unfairly targeted by police because of the color of their skin, and police believe they are unfairly judged by their communities because of the color of their uniforms, we have another bridge to cross."

Last June, the President and the Attorney General brought together 200 people for a two-day conference on police-community relations. This was a group of people who didn't often sit down together, who didn't know each other. We had representatives from the national civil rights groups, and representatives from the national police labor unions. We had community groups alongside representatives of the DEA and the INS. We had young people from New York City and police chiefs from small towns around the country. People wondered, justifiably, what was going to happen after we left that room, whether this would be just another well-meaning conference that didn't produce anything.

I'd like to describe for you some of the developments since then, to show that conferences such as the one we held last June can make a concrete difference in how the police and the community interact. At any given time we, along with the FBI, are investigating several hundred individual allegations of police misconduct for violations of criminal civil rights laws around the country. Since 1993, we have backed up local and state prosecutors by criminally prosecuting more than 360 individual law enforcement officers for willful violations of constitutional rights such as the use of excessive force. The prosecutions of the officers who brutalized Rodney King and Abner Louima are examples.

A second important—and more broad-based—tool in dealing with policing issues is our authority under the 1994 Crime Act to bring civil suits alleging patterns or practices of police misconduct. Our civil pattern and practice jurisdiction does not address misconduct by individual officers. It addresses systemic failures of police departments to provide proper supervision, to adequately discipline and train officers, and to prohibit racial profiling. Last December, for example, we filed a case accompanied by a consent decree against the New Jersey State Police based on admitted evidence of racial profiling on the State's highways against African-American and Hispanic drivers. In a model decree, New Jersey agreed to prohibit its state troopers from relying on race or national origin when making traffic stops, to document the race and national origin of all drivers stopped, to publicly disclose traffic stop statistics, to strengthen supervision, to provide better training, to institute an early warning system and to provide for monitoring.

In January of this year, we reached a similar agreement with the police department in Montgomery County, Maryland, concerning racial profiling and complaint procedures. That agreement, among other things, covers data collection on traffic stops. In that case, we were able to draft an agreement with the Montgomery County police department, and, importantly, the police union, that will improve the Department and the experience of motorists of Montgomery County. We have previously settled cases involving patterns or practices of use of excessive force and false arrests in Pittsburgh, Pennsylvania, and Steubenville, Ohio. We are litigating against Columbus, Ohio's police department. We are currently investigating a number of other police departments including Washington, D.C., Riverside, California, New Orleans, Louisiana, and, New York City in conjunction with the local U.S. Attorney's Office.

The Department also has encouraged voluntary efforts to address the problem of racial profiling. Last June, when the President and the Attorney General condemned racial profiling and recommended data collection, only three jurisdictions—San Jose, San Diego, and the State Patrol in North Carolina—had voluntarily agreed to collect traffic stop data. When we held our follow-up meeting on racial profiling and data collection in February of this year, there were over 100 jurisdictions who had begun or announced plans to collect data on traffic or pedestrian stops. These departments realize that finding out if there is a problem is the first step in addressing it. By providing information about the location, reasoning, and demographics of police enforcement patterns, data collection can shift the rhetoric surrounding racial profiling from accusations and anecdotal stories to a more rational, informed discussion about the appropriate allocation of police resources. Such data also can serve as a catalyst for substantive community-police discussion on priorities and effectiveness. In addition to sponsoring meetings where jurisdictions can share their experiences and learn from each other, as well as academic and police experts, the Department is funding the publication of a data collection resource guide that will make this information available to a wider audience. The guide should be available later this summer, and be incorporated into a Web site.

In keeping with these efforts, I would like to note the Department's efforts with respect to its own law enforcement components that, like state and local law enforcement, have been criticized for use of force and racial profiling. The Department of Justice believes that the legal principles we urge in our enforcement efforts should govern as well the operations of federal law enforcement components. We are pleased that the president has not only condemned police racial profiling generally, but issued an executive memorandum requiring federal law enforcement components to begin data collection and to analyze their own policies and procedures with respect to the use of race and ethnicity. Participating agencies include the DEA, the INS, the Customs Service, and the Park Police. We are seeking to put our own house in order.

In addition to direct efforts to remedy police misconduct, the Justice Department addresses problems in law enforcement through employment discrimination litigation. Over the years, we have brought hundreds of lawsuits that have helped lead to long-term change in the racial and gender makeup of our nation's law enforcement departments. Combating employment discrimination helps us combat police misconduct because ending exclusionary practices opens the talent pool. Police forces that reflect the diversity of the communities they serve also are better able to form positive working relationships with community members, leading to more effective law enforcement. When someone who grows up in a neighborhood becomes an officer there, he or she understands the people and knows the languages spoken there. There is less fear and mistrust, and that can lead to less misconduct. Police forces that are unrepresentative have been seen as forces of oppression.

The last aspect of our initiative to combat police misconduct and improve police-community relations are the many DOJ programs supporting community-oriented policing. Community policing is a philosophy of policing that seeks to improve public safety by involving the community in establishing police priorities, and involving

---

> *Police forces that reflect the diversity of the communities they serve also are better able to form positive working relationships with community members, leading to more effective law enforcement.*

---

police officers in the communities they serve. It includes creating partnerships between the police and institutions such as schools and religious institutions. In cities across this nation, police departments are encouraging officers to organize and participate in community activities, and developing ways for the community to participate in police decision-making.

Now let me turn to the second set of initiatives the Department has undertaken to strengthen the confidence of minority communities in the justice system—increasing the number of minority lawyers and those who provide legal services to minority communities. You probably are familiar with the ruling by the Fifth Circuit in Hopwood that the University of Texas Law School could not consider race or ethnicity in its admissions decisions, rejecting Justice Powell's opinion in the case, that diversity was a compelling justification for an affirmative action admissions program. This ruling prompted us to consider the Department's role in protecting the gains that have been made over the past thirty years in ensuring that racial and ethnic minorities are not denied the opportunity to attend law school and participate in the justice system.

As one response to the decision, the Attorney General sponsored a conference to which we invited 200 leaders from every sector of the legal profession to address the challenges race and ethnicity present to the legal profession. One of the most compelling arguments opposing the position expressed in was articulated at the conference by Professors Derek Bok and William Bowen, the authors of *The Shape of the River.* That landmark book dispelled many of the myths surrounding affirmative action in the undergraduate setting, including the claim that diversity admissions program harmed ill-prepared minority students. Bok and Bowen documented that minority students benefitted from such programs at elite institutions by every measure and, in fact, went on to greater civic participation than fellow white students. Bok and Bowen have moved the debate forward to the facts. They concluded that going to a race-blind admissions system in law school would have drastic effects. They examined the data and estimated what would happen if the top half of this nation's 173 law schools no longer considered race. The result, and it is truly astounding, is that the enrollment of African American and Latino students at those schools would drop to less than 2%.

To put it another way, but for diversity admissions programs, only a fraction of the minority lawyers now available for judicial appointments and other high government posts would have been trained at any of the top law schools in this country. Even with the law schools' current efforts to attract minority students, minority ethnic and racial groups continue to be present only in small numbers. Consider the following statistics:

a. Only 2% of all partners in the nation's largest and most-profitable law firms are racial minorities. In the 77 largest firms in New York City, 34 out of 4400 partners are African-American—a rate of three-quarters of one percent. In the 40 largest firms in Chicago, only 46 out of almost 3000 partners are African-American. One in ten of the nation's largest firms has no more than one minority lawyer.

b. Only eleven general counsels of Fortune 500 companies are minorities, and eight of them were named in the last three years. Overall, women comprise 37% of the nation's corporate counsel legal staff and racial minorities comprise 9%.

These troubling disparities continue to occur as one rises to higher and higher career plateaus. The percentage of minority partners at major law firms is minuscule, even compared to the percentage of minority associates. And among the pool of partners, barely half of African-American partners at large law firms hold equity stakes, as compared to 70% of their white counterparts. In short, our profession, which operates and staffs the justice system, does not look like our society.

A crucial issue for law schools, in law firms and at the Department of Justice, for all of us, is how do we define and measure merit? What really makes someone a good lawyer? This is something that everyone here needs to think about, and act upon. We have to move beyond what Judge Ruben Castillo of the District Court in Illinois called the "mirror, mirror on the wall philosophy," our tendency to like people who are like ourselves. When that happens, we perpetuate a closed system. And we lose out on the real value of diversity, which is that diversity makes us more effective.

Those of you who frequent our courts know that our jury pool is changing rapidly as our population becomes more diverse. A lawyer who doesn't understand that, who doesn't have experience working and learning with people of different races and backgrounds and languages, is not going to be as effective in persuading that jury as one who knows how to communicate with a diverse audience.

Identifying real merit is not easy. Certainly not as easy as looking at numbers. It takes real time and real effort to try and figure out who is going to make the most of an educational opportunity, or who is going to excel in corporate practice, or who is going to make a fair and effective prosecutor. But it is time well spent.

To ensure that governmental efforts to achieve diversity in education will not be outlawed, the Civil Rights Division has filed amicus briefs in several cases arguing that the Fourteenth Amendment permits state-supported colleges and elementary and secondary schools to use race as one factor to achieve the educational benefits of a diverse student body. We believe that diversity can be a compelling reason to utilize race as factor in admissions. We have answered challenges to diversity admissions programs at the University of Michigan and University of Washington, and to elementary and secondary schools in Maryland, Virginia, and New York. We may not have been as successful as we hoped in convincing the courts, but the jury is still out.

On the other hand, many of you know of the opinion a few years ago, extending to federal government contacting the strict scrutiny standards applicable to state and local affirmative action programs. Adarand was characterized by some as sounding the death knell for affirmative action in government contracting. However, two years ago Congress reauthorized two large programs for race conscious government contracting, recognizing discrimination against minority contractors justified such programs.

I believe that properly framed affirmative action in government programs will survive because it is needed as a matter of justice, but also of pragmaticism. As our society becomes more diverse it must also become inclusive or we will not 7long survive.

To that end, the president has issued a Call to Action to the legal profession. On July 20, 1999, the president called a group of 200 bar leaders to the East Room in the White House—the same room where, 36 years earlier, President Kennedy called a group of lawyers together to enlist them in the fight for equal justice when the very rule of law was being challenged. As the lawyers in 1963 answered President Kennedy's call, in part by forming the Lawyers Committee for Civil Rights, and working with organizations such as the NAACP LDF, President Clinton urged those assembled before him to step forward in the fight to dismantle the most stubborn obstacles to equal justice—poverty, unemployment, and continuing discrimination.

The president's Call to Action resulted in the formation of Lawyers for One America, a non-profit organization dedicated to working with lawyers, corporations, law firms, law schools, bar associations, civil rights groups, and public interest organizations to meet the president's challenge. Affiliated organizations include the American Corporate Counsel Association, the Minority Corporate Counsel Association, the National Bar Association, the Association of American Law Schools, the Association of the Bar of New York, and the National Association of Public Interest Law.

Lawyers for One America is working to create a database of successful practices and programs that are aimed at increasing diversity at all levels of the legal profession and expanding access to legal services. It is promoting these practices and programs through its extensive outreach network by means of several media, conferences, speeches, news articles, the Internet. This July, for example, Lawyers for One America will sponsor a day of coordinated pro bono work in several cities in order to raise awareness and to encourage such activity.

In order to appreciate the obstacles we as a profession face, one committee of Lawyers for One America is working to compile reliable statistics on the current composition of different tiers of the legal community, from law students to academics, associates to partners, law clerks to judges. Meanwhile, individual legal organizations are working one-on-one with Lawyers for One America to take their own steps towards meeting the president's challenge. At the Justice Department, we have developed an eight-point plan to recruit, hire and promote a more diverse pool of attorneys, we are revising our departmental pro bono policy, and we are reaching out to other federal agencies to encourage similar changes. Lawyers for One America is preparing to deliver a comprehensive report of its activities to the president this fall.

The president called upon the legal profession to "recommit [them] selves to fighting discrimination, to revitalizing our poorest communities, and to giving people an opportunity to serve in law firms who would not otherwise have it." And the president called upon the legal profession to "set the best possible example," to tear down the "walls in our hearts and in our habits."

Thank you.

II. Election Reform

Vote Theft 2000

Selecting Our Leaders Fairly and Honestly[1]

Julia Hughes Jones

Retired Arkansas State Auditor, 1981–95; born Camden, AR, September 9, 1939; attended Texas Woman's University, 1957–58, and University of Arkansas, Fayetteville, 1958–60 and 1961; University of Arkansas, Little Rock, 1983; attended Institute for Court Management, Denver, CO, 1976–77; attended John F. Kennedy School of Government's State and Local Government Executive Program, Harvard University, 1981; chief investigator, prosecuting attorney's office, Little Rock, 1973–76; circuit clerk, Pulaski County, AR, 1977–79; project director, Association of Arkansas Counties, 1979–80; U.S. Senate candidate, 1992; speeches published in Vital Speeches of the Day, *1992, 1998, and 2000; authored "Women in Politics" in* Encyclopedia of the Future, *1996; featured on* Fox News Network, *1999, NET Political News Talk Network, and* American Investigator News Show, *1997 and 1998.*

Editors' introduction: Drawing upon her years of experience working with voter registration at the state level, Ms. Jones described for some thirty members of the Jacksonville Women's Monday Book Club how "the American voting process" could be guided in "a new direction." Ms. Jones was the first aspiring author to address the group and was asked particularly to speak about the nation's current election problems. This meeting was held in the home of Ms. Audrey McCullum, retired realtor and arts enthusiast. The members were highly attentive, asked questions about the 2000 presidential election "squabble," and expressed gratitude to the speaker for informing them about the election process. Ms. Jones warned that, "if we are not allowed to select our leaders fairly and honestly, we can no longer have a republican democracy."

Julia Hughes Jones's speech: Thank you for inviting me to speak to you today about one of the chapters in my unfinished book about politics, power and propaganda. As you know, I served as an elected statewide constitutional officer in Arkansas from 1981 until retirement in 1995.

---

1. Delivered in Jacksonville, Florida, on November 27, 2000, at noon. Reprinted with permission of Julia Hughes Jones.

The subject of the chapter I am reviewing today concerns the election process, a timely topic since the winner of the 2000 presidential election is still being debated. The chapter's thesis is a simple concept:

Vote stealing is the theft of the right of voters to choose those who lead them.

I intend to show how you, as informed women, can help steer the American voting process in a new direction at the third millennium. The last section includes tips for what you can do to help stop vote fraud and what to look for if foul play is suspected.

I am not an attorney, but to survive Arkansas politics and just do my job I had to learn more than I ever wanted to know about constitutional and statutory law and the judicial and legislative processes.

> *Vote stealing is the theft of the right of voters to choose those who lead them.*

I confess I have an executive branch mentality in seeing what is happening in Florida. I also confess to being a Republican (and a former Democrat) with an independent attitude that includes using common sense rather than following a party line without question.

Between 1981 and 1995 I was the only elected executive branch Auditor in the country with voter registration duties. Most other states placed that job with the Secretaries of State. My job was to assist the 75 county clerks in their duty as voter registrars by distributing voter registration affidavits and by reporting annually on the status of voter registration.

These duties were placed under the state Auditor by a people's direct initiative to amend the state constitution and approved by voters in 1965. The amendment effectively replaced the poll tax as a requirement for voting. The story told by the women who sponsored this initiative was that the Arkansas Secretary of State at the time was not to be trusted with voter registration.

Because of my executive branch experience, I have observed with great interest the attacks on Florida Secretary of State Katherine Harris. The attempt to take away her executive branch discretionary powers plainly shows a blatant disregard for the separation of powers between the branches of government. It is true that the executive branch was the least trusted by the country's founders. It is true the founders created enough checks and balances between the branches to avoid the monarchical abuses of power Americans had suffered under King George of England, an executive branch official himself.

Regardless of historically perceived executive branch abuse, each branch of American government is equal in power to the others. There are built-in checks and balances to avoid the usurpation by one branch on another. Rewriting the law in the middle of the process is not an acceptable check-and-balance. Character attacks on the executive branch official exercising her duty under the law is not an acceptable check-and-balance.

If the Florida Legislature has been deficient in passing election laws, the judicial branch is obligated to overcome those deficiencies *after the fact* and not in the middle of the election process. When a law states precisely that an official has discretionary powers to make a determination of validity, any attempt to circumvent that official's exercise of power is encroachment. What is shocking about this entire fiasco is the total disregard for the people's elected Secretary of State, a constitutional officer, and the obtrusive attempt to encourage the judicial branch to control the executive's actions *after the action has been taken.*

In a civilized society, the rule of law means that rules must be followed. If the rules are no longer acceptable to the majority, then they must be changed by the legislative branch, not by a court of law, and certainly not in the middle of the process of an executive's acting on the law. The laws in effect at the time of the election are the rule of law, as it has customarily been interpreted and acted upon. The rule of law does not include a retroactive rewriting or reinterpretation of the law to suit the current circumstances.

> *What is shocking about this entire fiasco is the total disregard for the people's elected Secretary of State.*

Florida's chief election official is endowed by law with the right to make a judgment as to validity of election returns for certification. When one group dislikes her decision and takes her to court, it implies that she is incapable of exercising her executive branch responsibilities. Florida voters found her to be capable and the Florida legislature wrote the laws she must follow.

As citizens of the longest running republican democracy in history, Americans are now being forced to look closely at the way elections are conducted. The entire public has been caught up in a squabble that has brought charges of election stealing, tyranny, abuse of power, incompetent administering of the law, and outright autocratic recounting until the proper result is reached. (It has been duly noted by some that recounting the vote until it was acceptable is the way Hitler took power.)

The American sense of humor is always at play where elections are concerned and the Internet is replete with the Florida joke of the day. Public speakers have always told humorous anecdotes about well-meaning citizens who go to church every time the doors are open and yet think absolutely nothing is wrong with manipulating election results "for the good of the state." The question we must ask is: "Are we short-changing ourselves by laughing at something as serious as the elective process?" Frankly, there is nothing wrong with a dose of humor in a critical situation. The problem comes when election officials believe the public *expects* hanky-panky in the elections process.

Stolen elections perpetuate corrupt politicians and maintain the status quo.

All the taxpayers and voters who claim to be cynical about government and disgusted with elected officials must remember that "pay to play" and "playing the game" are two metaphors politicians understand completely. These politicians know they have to "play the game" as it is played (follow the rules from the top, not from the bottom), and they have to require those who seek favor to "pay to play" (if you want something from government, you give money), or the game is over for the politician.

Stolen elections perpetuate corrupt politicians and maintain the status quo.

What this means is that the controlling agents in society keep out the newcomers who refuse to play the game under the current rules, and there can never be a change in attitude about whose interests must be served first.

In the old days before electronic voting, it took collaboration between local election officials to steal elections and no one ever knew. Nowadays, it requires only one official and one software program designer. The official involved does not even have to be involved in the elections process. Contracts are awarded by local government entities and there is usually only one official in charge of putting out the specifications for bids. The key here is in finding out just what secret conditions are attached to the contract. No contractor can afford to resist the lure of a signed and sealed contract, no matter the secret conditions that may be required.

Public accountability and ethics laws do not extend to computer programmers and election equipment companies. Software programs can be designed to double-count or even triple-count certain ballots selected by frequency and type of vote. Software tweaking cannot be detected because electronic voting does not leave a paper trail, and computer programming is rarely understood by anyone other than the programmer.

One final point about vote stealing potential at the millennium involves advertising claims from the election equipment companies. When a company advertises their products as being used worldwide, questions can be raised as to which countries are purchasing their equipment. If these customers are "people's" democracies or one-party countries, are they under the control of a single tyrant or an elite group of tyrants? If so, you can bet the equipment or software can be tweaked in favor of the controlling authorities.

In the end, the stealing of elections is not about partisan political behavior or even political issues. Elections are stolen as a *control* mechanism. The relatively new and fraud-friendly "motor-voter" registration law helps those in power to retain control of the process. What is meant by "fraud-friendly"?

The failure to require identification to register and the automatic approval of mail-in applicants invites deception.

Lack of purging on a regular basis is the biggest error of all in this law. Dead people and convicted felons are never removed from voter rolls unless the agencies involved actively monitor death notices and criminal court records. Since most voter registrars in this country are elected clerks with many other responsibilities, there is seldom enough time and effort to purge either the cemetery vote or the prison vote.

For voters who suspect hanky-panky in their own elections, the following steps can be taken to assure honest elections in your country.

Find out what type of voting equipment is used in your county and exactly who is in control of it and who contracted for it.

Determine the backgrounds of all individuals involved in the running of this equipment and find out who they are beholden to for their jobs.

Call or write the Federal Election Commission and the Bureau of Standards in Washington, D.C., for information about the type of voting and tabulating equipment in use by your county.

Find out who the election equipment company's principals are and check their backgrounds for criminal records, political ties, and complaints about service.

Ask for a demonstration of the equipment's audit trail to ascertain that results can be verified within a few days of the election. If your election officials claim there is no money to pay for this, volunteer your efforts in getting it done for free by concerned citizens. Don't take no for an answer.

If your county is set up for computer voting or tabulation or some other form of mechanization where it is difficult to know if pre-programming of winners has taken place, work to get passage of a law requiring a percentage of ballots to be either counted by hand or otherwise verified after each election to test accuracy of the process.

Election equipment companies can be required by law to build in an audit trail. If they refuse, change the equipment or see that they are not paid until they make the required changes.

If votes are counted at the precinct level, there is usually a posting of the tally on the door of the precinct after the count. Collect the information from each precinct to make certain results are not switched at the central tallying point.

Finally, compare the total number of votes recorded with the number of people checked off as present at the polls. Any discrepancy is worthy of a challenge.

Candidates and voters alike must always be on the look-out for signs of tampering with election results, regardless of how ethical the people are who conduct the elections. Tip-offs that foul play has occurred include the following.

If the number of absentee ballots is out of line with past trends, demand an audit.

If a leading candidate's vote totals suddenly drop behind due to a "computer breakdown" or "malfunction," find out just what happened.

If a large scale voter registration campaign takes place within months of the election, fraudulent ballots can amount to as much as twenty percent of the vote in those areas, especially if absentee ballots are legally given to someone other than the actual voter.

If "swing-ballots" are mentioned as the determining factor in an election, check them out. False registrations are popular in the south and in third-world countries that bother to require registration. It is called the "cemetery vote" in Arkansas but has been labeled as "swing-ballots" in other states. Duplicate registrations in several counties allow one person to vote in all counties where registered. (Don't believe for a minute that counties are too far apart mileage-wise; absentee voting is the preferred choice in this.)

If "bounty-hunters" are being paid in your area to register voters, you can count on illegal registrations. Aliens in particular are registered under the pretense that the laws have changed to allow it.

Finally, when ballots are examined in hand recounts the fact that no vote was cast in a presidential race is not proof of voter illiteracy or intent. Just because the rest of the ballot is voted a straight party line does not mean the voter intended to do so in the presidential race. After all, there is no place on American ballots for "None of the above"—and voters can exercise their right to vote by *not* voting at times.

In closing let me remind you that *vote stealing is the theft of the right of voters to choose those who lead them.* If we are not allowed to select our leaders fairly and honestly, we can no longer have a republican democracy.

Making Democracy Work[2]

Carolyn Jefferson-Jenkins, Ph.D.

President, League of Women Voters of the United States, 1998– , and chair of the League of Women Voters Education Fund; born in Cleveland, OH, September 19, 1952; B.A. in social science and education, Western College (Miami University), Oxford, OH, 1974; M.Ed. in administration and supervision, John Carroll University, OH, 1981; Ph.D. in urban education and administration, Cleveland State University, 1991; principal in the Cleveland and Cleveland Heights, University Heights Public School Systems, 1993–95; author, One Man One Vote: the History of the African-American Vote in the United States, *1991; first African-American woman to head the League of Women Voters; Outstanding Young Woman in America Award; National Coalition of Black Civic Participation's Civic Leadership Award; Distinguished Alumni Award in Civic Leadership, Cleveland State University.*

Editors' introduction: Dr. Carolyn Jefferson-Jenkins spoke to some 100 persons attending a public forum organized by the Commonwealth Club of California, the nation's oldest and largest public affairs forum. In attendance at this meeting, sponsored by the Club's San Francisco office, were members of that organization and students from the University of Berkeley. Concerned about problems with elections ranging from "administration" to "constitutional issues," Dr. Jefferson-Jenkins maintained that "we need new and effective standards to ensure that voters' rights will be fully protected."

Dr. Carolyn Jefferson-Jenkins's speech: Good Evening! It is indeed a pleasure to be able to speak to you this evening on a topic that has captured the public's attention for the past four months and threatens to hold our attention through the elections of 2004. That topic, the organizing theme for my remarks this evening, is *Making Democracy Work*—for all citizens, for all voters.

On behalf of the League of Women Voters of the United States Board of Directors, the League of Women Voters Education Fund Board of Trustees, our 50 state Leagues, the Leagues in the District of Columbia, U.S. Virgin Islands and Puerto Rico and our 1000 local Leagues, I would like to thank George Dobbins, program director of the Commonwealth Club, for providing this opportunity to discuss this important issue. I would also like to thank the League of

---

2. Delivered in California the morning of February 21, 2001. Reprinted with permission of Carolyn Jefferson-Jenkins.

Women Voters of San Francisco, in particular, President Hollie Thier and Vice President Patricia Mitchell, for inviting me to the Bay area.

I would be remiss if I did not recognize members of other Leagues who have joined us this evening and I ask them to stand at this time and be recognized.

On February 14, 2001, the League celebrated its 81st Anniversary. During these 81 years, we have encouraged the informed and active participation of citizens in government, worked to increase understanding of major public policy issues and influenced public policy through education and advocacy. We will continue to do so for the next 81 years—as Election 2000 has underscored the need for our continued work.

> *Election 2000 has lifted the veil on the many problems that confront our nation's election system.*

Founded by activists who secured voting rights for women, the League has always worked to promote the values and processes of representative government—protecting and enhancing voting rights for all Americans, assuring opportunities for citizen participation and working for open, accountable, representative and responsive government at every level. These efforts all reflect the deeply held convictions of the League of Women Voters.

You may learn more about the League of Women Voters, its programs and its positions by accessing our Web site at *www.lwv.org*.

One of many articles printed in the months following election 2000 accurately stated, "Our national civics lesson is over. But what, if anything, have we learned from the closest presidential election in more than a century?"

We've learned a lot. Now, whether we do something about it is the more important question.

From the very beginning, the right to vote has been a subject of continuous debate. Benjamin Franklin said in *Wit and Sentiment* (1828):

> Today a man owns jackass worth fifty dollars and he is entitled to vote; but before the next election the jackass dies. The man in the meantime has become more experienced, his knowledge of the principles of government, and his acquaintance with mankind, are more extensive, and he is therefore better qualified to make a proper selection of rulers—but the jackass is dead and the man cannot vote. Now, gentlemen, pray inform me, in whom is the right of suffrage? In the man or in the jackass?

Election 2000 has lifted the veil on the many problems that confront our nation's election system, from election administration issues, such as counting mechanisms and ballot design, to constitutional issues, illustrated in the Electoral College. These issues fall into two basic categories: one, where the problems and solutions are clear so that we can move forward quickly and effectively and two, where there is no agreement on either the scope or nature of the problems and their solutions.

The League of Women Voters believes in representative government and in individual liberties as established in the Constitution of the United States. We believe that democratic government depends upon the informed and active participation of its citizens and requires that governmental bodies protect the citizens' right to know by giving adequate notice of proposed actions, holding meetings and making public records accessible. Further, we believe that every citizen should be protected in the exercise of these rights.

Fundamental to this participation is the citizens' right to vote. In order to increase participation, the League believes that election officials have the responsibility for encouraging the exercise of the vote, for promoting citizen confidence in and understanding of the electoral process and for providing equal access to the ballot.

Election officials have the responsibility for encouraging the exercise of the vote.

To say that obstacles to voting in the United States are only related to election 2000 would be a misstatement. Let me show you why.

Would everyone please stand? If you are unable to stand, forgive me for this discriminatory statement, and we will find some other way for you to participate.

Everyone who does not meet voter requirements as I state them must sit down as they are called out.

1. Anyone who was not 18 years old by November 7, 2000 must sit down. (In 1971, the 26th Amendment gave citizens over the age of 18 the right to vote.)
2. Anyone not living in the same place for over a year must sit down. (Before passage of the 1970 Voting Rights Act, most states had residency requirements of anywhere from 3 months to 2 years. The 1970 law abolished any residency requirement of more than 30 days.)
3. Anyone who cannot read or write English well enough to pass a literacy test must sit down. (The 1970 Voter Rights Act abolished literacy tests.)
4. Anyone who is not fluent in English must sit down. (The 1965 Voter Rights Act made it possible for Spanish speaking citizens to vote.)
5. Anyone who does not have $1.00 must sit down. (In 1964, the 24th Amendment abolished the poll tax of $1 or $2 that many states had required.)

6. Anyone who is not male must sit down. (In 1920, the 19th Amendment gave women the right to vote.)
7. Anyone who is not white must sit down. (In 1870, the 15th amendment forbade denial of citizenship on the basis of race.)
8. Anyone who does not own property must sit down. (By 1821, most states had abolished property or tax requirements.)
9. All non-Protestants must sit down. If Catholic, Jewish, Muslim, etc., you must sit down. (In the early years of the federacy, in most states, being Protestant was a requirement.)

Who is left who had the right to vote? How did you feel when you were excluded from voting? How did you feel about those who had the right to vote?

Most citizens show little interest in the process . . . because they do not recognize the extent to which the current election system impairs the right of all Americans to engage in self-government.

Several members of Congress have drafted or are drafting legislation to reform election administration. The League is working closely with these offices to craft workable approaches.

We comment whenever possible on other forward-looking election reform issues. We have been commenting on these issues since the 1970s.

Reports from our previous studies, *Removing Administrative Obstacles to Voting before the Election and beyond* and *Administrative Obstacles to Voting,* published by the LWVEF in 1972, underscore that this is not a new issue.

According to an old adage, it's the squeaky wheel that gets the oil. Clearly, when the malfunctions or inequities of a system creak too loudly and too long, reformers move in.

Problems concerning registration places, registration hours, deputy registrars, registration lists, administrative resources, voter information and polling places need to be addressed.

The need for election reform through federal legislation has been documented and endorsed by several committees of national prominence. A model state election code is also being developed.

In addition to changes in election laws, there is a need for changes in administrative practices of local and state election officials. For purposes of these remarks, I define administrative practices as standards, procedures and structures set up to implement state election laws.

Most citizens show little interest in the process not because they dismiss its importance, but simply because they do not recognize the extent to which the current election system impairs the right of all Americans to engage in self-government. The public generally believes that the system has worked well in the past and that it will work well in the future.

Regrettably, the present election system has not worked well. It still bears the mark of the forces which originally gave it birth at the turn of the last century: fear of the then widespread corruption and fraud at the polls and a desire to control the voting participation of millions of European immigrants who threatened the political status quo.

Although these particular forces have largely ceased to exist, the system remains saddled with many unnecessarily restrictive laws

To what extent can electoral reform occur within the context of existing law?

and exclusionary procedures. It has become an administrative maze in which many of the abuses it was designed to prevent can, in fact, be more easily hidden and through which the average citizens must painstakingly grope in order to exercise their fundamental right to the franchise.

Fear of fraud is often advanced in opposition to proposed reform of the present election system. It could be argued, however, that such abuses are a function of community mores and will exist in some communities no matter what election procedures are established. More noteworthy, it would seem, is the fraud perpetuated on the American people by a system which excludes millions of eligible voters from the electoral process in the name of preventing a few dishonestly cast votes.

To what extent can electoral reform occur within the context of existing law? To what degree do current state election laws affect the administrative behavior of election officials?

In a few areas of registration and voting, the law is specific. Residency requirements and closing dates for registration are examples. Although the capacity of administrators and local officials to act independently is considerably limited in these instances, they CAN determine the impact of these laws by the vigor with which they make these requirements known and encourage citizens to meet them.

Local officials may be even more powerful where the law is merely permissive. State statutes frequently allow, but do not require, the following: precinct registration, Saturday and/or evening regulation hours and the authorization of deputy registrars.

In addition to their influence in areas where the law is stated in broad or permissive terms, local officials are able to influence the electoral process in matters where the law is silent. Although the law may not require, suggest or forbid it, an election official might provide information to citizens concerning the election, might conduct extensive training programs for all poll workers and might provide bilingual clerks where needed. To a large extent, local officials retain their discretionary powers by default.

The following list represents a sampling of the problems:

- Perception of registration and voting problems;
- Residency requirements;
- Complex registration procedures;
- Complex absentee voting procedures;
- Inconvenient registration hours;
- Distant and inconvenient places of registration;
- Complicated voting procedures;
- Inconvenient polling hours;
- Positioning candidates names on the ballot; and
- Ensuring the proper functioning of voting machines.

Our biggest challenges right now are in the areas of Election Reform, Campaign Finance reform and the Electoral College. We are tackling these challenges at all levels because we firmly believe that representative government is the foundation of our democratic process.

The 2000 election highlighted the need to improve the way that ballots are cast and counted in many areas of the country. The election called attention to the fact that the federal government makes no meaningful financial contribution to defray the costs of federal elections.

On January 29, 2001, twenty-five public interest, civil rights, labor and disability rights organizations released the key elements that we believe must be included in any election reform legislation in the 107 Congress. The organizations' statement of principles came as members of Congress were introducing legislation to redress the problems in election administration exposed by the 2000 election. President Bush has also expressed an interest in election reform.

In a letter to members of the House and Senate, the organizations urged that Congress act quickly to develop and pass truly nonpartisan election reform legislation that will garner majority support from members of both political parties. The letter indicated our belief that several key elements must be included in any bill aimed at reforming election administration. While many of us believe that more is needed, these essential elements may provide a basis for avoiding partisan controversy and moving ahead quickly.

We support legislation that

1. Creates a substantial, multi-year federal grants program to upgrade election technologies, including

    • Improved voting equipment and associated counting mechanisms, and

    • State-wide technologies on a uniform basis, such as computerized voter registration lists;

2. Protects the Voting Rights Act and the National Voter Registration Act—known as motor voter—while ensuring that any activities under the new legislation are consistent with these existing laws;

3. Sets federally-approved "best practices" for grant-eligible technologies that include standards that ensure

    • Accessibility and convenience for the voter, including voters and disabilities,

    • Accuracy, including safeguards for maintaining voter rolls, and

    • Nondiscrimination, including full participation for language, racial and ethnic minorities and people with disabilities;

4. Includes criteria to ensure that jurisdictions with the most significant problems receive needed funding.

In addition to the League of Women Voters, this letter was signed by such groups as the National Council of La Raza, NAACP Legal Defense Fund, National Organization on Disability, Public Campaign, National Education Association, Common Cause and National Urban League, to name a few.

In all the state Leagues, members are addressing issues on a state by state basis. For example, in Alabama, the League sits on a Commission looking at procedures and machines; in Alaska, they are helping to set up guidelines for primary elections; in Connecticut, they are looking at absentee ballots, roll maintenance, poll worker training and equipment; in Indiana, the focus is on election voting systems and statewide computerized voter registration; in Georgia, the emphasis is on uniformity of equipment and training across the state; and in Maryland, uniformity of voting machinery is a top priority. The League of Women Voters supports uniform national voting qualifications and procedures for presidential elections.

The League has received numerous requests to explain its 1970 position on the Electoral College. The study, which took 2 years, commenced immediately after the 1968 election and resulted in the following position:

- The League of Women Voters supports the national direct popular vote method to elect the President and Vice President of the United States.

- The League of Women Voters believes that the direct popular vote method for electing the President and Vice President is essential to representative government and should include a provision for a national run-off in the event no candidate (President and Vice President) receive 40% of the popular vote.

- The League of Women Voters believes that the Electoral College should be abolished and that, only as a last resort, should reform of the present Electoral College method be undertaken. Such reform, if undertaken, should include: allocating the electoral votes proportionally to the popular vote within each state and the District of Columbia abolishing the office of elector or binding electors in the U.S. Constitution and improving the congressional-contingent election procedure.

With respect to the challenges represented by Campaign Finance Reform, Senate leaders have decided to bring campaign finance reform to the floor of the Senate during the end of March. Meaningful campaign finance reform is not just about politicians and money. It is about a more representative decision-making process.

The League supports the Campaign Finance Reform bill as introduced by Senators John McCain and Russ Feingold. Their bill would:

1. Ban soft money by closing the loophole that allows unlimited contributions to political parties from corporations, unions and wealthy individuals;
2. Prohibit corporate and union spending on "sham issue" advocacy that mentions federal candidates within 60 days of an election;
3. Require full disclosure of spending on "sham issue" advocacy and the large individual donors who pay for them.

And let's not forget the citizens of the District of Columbia who still do not have full congressional voting rights.

Our election administration systems are in dire need of repair. Unfortunately, the federal government does not pay its fair share of the costs of federal elections. Last year, the nation saw the results of that neglect.

The goal of election reform *must* be that the vote of every American citizen will count. The principles give us the criteria by which every federal election reform proposal must be judged.

The 2000 election made it clear that we need new and effective standards to ensure that voters' rights will be fully protected.

At the dawn of the 21st century, in the most vibrant democracy in history, we must address the persistent lack of attention and available resources that conspire to bar people—any people—from equal protection in the electoral process.

Antiquated voting machinery, ballot systems that confuse the voter and insufficient numbers of machines so that voters have to wait hours in line are just some of the problems that need to be addressed.

In conclusion, there is good news! More people than ever are learning about the democratic process. But, *Making Democracy Work* for all still eludes us.

New challenges bring new solutions.

As Benjamin Franklin stated, ladies and gentlemen, "In whom is the right of suffrage? In the man or in the jackass?" Our response to this national dilemma will tell.

I thank you.

Regarding Election Reform[3]

Scott Harshbarger

President and Chief Executive Officer of Common Cause, 1999– ; graduate of Harvard College, 1964; graduate of Harvard Law School, 1968; the first General Counsel to the Massachusetts State Ethics Commission, 1978–79; has taught at Boston University Law School, 1980– ; Middlesex County District Attorney, 1983–91; Massachusetts Attorney General, 1991–99; President, National Association of Attorneys General, 1996; Democratic nominee for Governor of Massachusetts, 1998; visiting professor, Harvard Law School; Hadley Professor of Criminal Justice and Law, Northeastern University.

Editors' introduction: Common Cause, founded in 1970, has focused on reducing the influence of money in politics, establishing high standards of government integrity, and ensuring government accountability. To those ends, President Scott Harshbarger testified before the second public hearing sponsored by the National Commission on Federal Election Reform, convened in the Lyndon Baines Johnson Library. The commission, organized by the Miller Center of Public Affairs and the Century Foundation, convened four public hearings across the United States, featuring experts in the field, elected leaders, interest group representatives, and academic scholars, to recommend ways to improve the accuracy and fairness of federal elections.

Scott Harshbarger's speech: Good morning. I am Scott Harshbarger, President and CEO of Common Cause, a citizens' advocacy group for open, accountable, and democratic government with some 200,000 members nationwide. I am also the President of the Common Cause Education Fund (CCEF)—our newly formed 501c(3) research and public education arm. On behalf of both Common Cause and the Common Cause Education Fund, I want to thank the National Commission on Election Reform for this opportunity to testify before you today on the problems with our election systems that were exposed so dramatically last November, and on policy solutions to move us ever closer to the ideal of "one-person, one-vote."

In its more than 30 years as a 501c(4) lobbying organization, Common Cause has been an aggressive proponent for democratic reforms of our political process. At the local, state, and federal level, we have played a lead role on campaign finance issues, legislative- and executive-branch ethics rules, reapportionment and redistrict-

---

3. Delivered in Austin, Texas, the morning of May 24, 2001. Reprinted with permission of Scott Harshbarger and Philip D. Zelikow, National Commission on Federal Election Reform.

ing, and other election-related laws like same-day registration and motor voter. We also have been key partners in civil rights and voting rights coalitions, and have worked to energize and mobilize all citizens to participate in our democracy.

Rooted in the core values that this historical mission and agenda reflects, we applaud the work that the Commission is doing to develop and recommend sound reforms to the way elections for public office are administered and conducted in this country. With thousands of grassroots activists across the country, chapters in most state capitals, and a wealth of experience in building the broad-based coalitions that are necessary to achieve democratic reforms, Common Cause is ready and well equipped to serve as a lead participant in election reform efforts at every level of government. If your final report addresses the broad set of election reform issues that speak directly to the health of our democracy—reforms aimed at re-engaging citizens in our political process—Common Cause is prepared to lead an aggressive push for implementation of your recommendations on Capitol Hill and in states legislatures throughout the country.

The formation of a unified and broad-based citizens' coalition will be critical to realizing election reform at all levels of government, as it was recently in the passage of campaign finance reform in the U.S. Senate. Common Cause already has joined many of the budding election reform partnerships and coalitions that have sprung into existence in the early months of this year. One partnership that I'd like to mention here because it relates directly to the work of this Commission is with the Fels Center of Government at the University of Pennsylvania. We have had discussions with them about their proposal for a "Voting Fairness Index" that would be compiled periodically at the state level. This index would measure voting accuracy and fairness. Common Cause's state chapters would play important roles in compiling the data that would be aggregated into an index and state ranking, as well as in using the index to encourage each state to improve its electoral process. As such, we envision that both Common Cause and the Fels Center would be engaged in activities that would follow up the work of this Commission. Indeed, we would welcome additional ideas from your Commission as to what we could do on a continuing basis to further our shared goal of improving our country's democracy.

In recent years, Common Cause has focused the majority of its resources and energies on campaign finance reform. We have made this choice not because we believe that the corrupting and undemocratic influence of money on our political process represents the only area in which reform is needed, but because we believe campaign finance is the most urgently needed area of political reform. Our democracy is based on the principle of political equality for all voting-age citizens. Current laws jeopardize this fundamental principle by allowing those with vast financial resources to translate their economic power into disproportionate political power. A significant part of the work toward improved elections would be left undone if we made voting systems more reliable and accessible, but continued to allow great disparities in campaign resources to determine the electoral winners in advance, leaving voters without a real choice between viable candidates.

> *We can begin to see the true nature of the crisis of the 2000 elections as a crisis of democracy.*

While I know the Commission does not intend to focus on specific campaign finance reform proposals in its deliberations and recommendations, I hope you will acknowledge in your report that our current corrupting campaign finance system has played a key role in destroying citizen confidence in our political process and in depressing citizen participation in it, including participation in voting itself. Because our current campaign finance laws have such a corrosive effect on democratic principles and rights, comprehensive and far-reaching reform of those laws must be part and parcel of any effort to revitalize citizen faith and participation in our electoral and legislative systems.

Just as the issue of money in politics profoundly impacts the vitality of key democratic values, so do the key election reform issues that we are here to discuss today. I fear that the recent crisis with our elections has been framed far too narrowly as a crisis of technology and complicated bureaucratic procedures. I believe this is a key reason why public momentum for reform has waned somewhat in recent months. We must remind the public, the press, and ourselves what is really at stake in matters like voting machinery, ballot designs, registration rules, and voter list maintenance. These matters may seem arcane, but they have direct implications for voting rights and citizen participation in our political process. In recognizing this, we can begin to see the true nature of the crisis of the 2000 elections as a crisis of democracy. If we treat the debacle of the 2000 elections as anything less, we will fail to respond with the energy and creativity that the situation demands.

Having said that election reform must not be narrowly framed as a technological issue, I do believe replacing inadequate voting equipment is a critical starting point for reform efforts. The 2000 elections rattled the confidence of American voters that their votes will be counted, even if they join the unacceptably small percentage of their fellow citizens who actually go to the polls. If citizen confidence in our election systems were the only thing at stake, the expense of replacing outmoded machines with state-of-the-art equipment would be worth incurring. Of course, voter confidence is not the only thing at stake. This is not simply a matter of perceptions, but of realities too. As Common Cause pointed out in a lawsuit filed in California with the American Civil Liberties Union and other organizations and individuals, unreliable equipment denies the citizens who use it the equal protection under the law that the Fourteenth Amendment to the U.S. Constitution guarantees. In California, jurisdictions using two types of pre-scored punch-card voting machines—the VotoMatic and the Pollstar machine—experienced average combined undervotes and overvotes double the average error rates of any other type of voting system used in the state. To make matters worse, minority populations used these machines disproportionately, placing yet another hurdle in front of those who have been denied their rights historically. The suit in which we are a plaintiff demands that the Secretary of State of California decertify those machines for use in his state.

> *It is appropriate for our elected representatives to set broad policy principles and standards for new voting equipment.*

While technology specialists and voting experts currently work to determine the specific voting machines that will best serve our democracy into the future, we believe it is appropriate for our elected representatives to set broad policy principles and standards for new voting equipment. Common Cause supports legislative language to this effect that has been included in two bills that have been introduced in the U.S. Senate. The standards in these bills include requiring voting machines to: 1) allow voters to verify their votes and make changes, 2) notify voters of over- or under-votes and offer the opportunity to correct those potential errors, 3) provide audit capacity through the production of a record of each vote, and 4) meet error-rate minimums to be determined by a blue-ribbon study commission. Voting machines meeting these standards would certainly address most of the problems raised last November.

In addition to making sure that votes are fairly and accurately counted when cast, we need to make sure that voters can get to the voting booth in a reasonable amount of time in the first place. News stories following the November election reported frustrated would-be voters in Michigan, Missouri, New York, Wisconsin, and elsewhere leaving polling places in anger—without having voted—because the lines to vote were excessively long. These lines, which for some constituted a *de facto* denial of voting rights, resulted from a variety of problems: machines broke down, polling places ran out of ballots, not enough election volunteers showed up to work, and some jurisdictions were unprepared on many levels for the high voter turnout they experienced. We must press state and local governments to correct this terrible wrong by investing the necessary resources in this process that is so central to our democracy. And because of the equal protection implications, Congress must also recognize its responsibility, by considering the potential for enforceable minimum standards for polling places and by providing resources directly where they are needed. We should also look for ways to entice employers to encourage their employees to work at the polls on election day.

In addition to faulty machines and resource deficiencies, I believe the two most disturbing violations of voting rights and equal protection in our last election were 1) the procedural blunders that left many eligible voters off the voting rolls, and 2) the policy in some dozen states of permanently disenfranchising ex-felons who already have paid their debt to society.

In many places around the country, registered voters were turned away from the polls because their names were left off or removed from the voting rolls. In Florida, to take the most well-known example, a deficient system for purging ineligible voters from the rolls resulted in the names of many qualified voters being "scrubbed" from the list. In other places, state and local officials apparently failed in their responsibilities under the National Voting Rights Act of 1993—the so-called motor voter law—to effectively process registrations submitted with drivers' license applications or in other interactions with government agencies. At a minimum, we can address this disaster by creating a national standard guaranteeing voters in every state the right to cast provisional ballots in cases in which there is a dispute over their registration.* But we must aim higher than the minimum. With the technology available to us today, we certainly have the means to all but guarantee that eligible voters—and only eligible voters—appear on the rolls on election day. Federal financial support and technical guidance may be required by some jurisdictions that have struggled to efficiently and effectively maintain voter rolls. However, we must not fail to put

---

* This right could be part of a Voters' Bill of Rights that some have proposed. This Bill of Rights would be posted prominently in every polling place and distributed to voters as a part of other public voter education activities carried out by government agencies.

forth the necessary resources and develop the necessary know-how, because egregious harm is done when even a single legal voter is denied the right to cast a ballot.

Such harm is done millions of times over each election day in the dozen states that permanently disenfranchise citizens who committed a crime sometime in the past but now have paid their debt to society. A 1998 study by Human Rights Watch and The Sentencing Project estimated that 1.4 million Americans in those states who have served out their sentences are permanently disenfranchised. In Florida alone, according to their estimates, nearly one-third of all voting-age African American men in the state were barred from the polls in November 2000. Stripping one of the most fundamental rights from these citizens in perpetuity is intolerable and un-Ameri-

---

Those holding the highest federal offices in the nation are elected with support from only a fraction of American adults.

---

can. The Connecticut state legislature has come to this realization, recently sending a bill to end the disenfranchisement of ex-felons to the Governor's desk where it currently awaits his signature. We hope the legislatures in the remaining states will follow Connecticut's lead, and abolish this unjust policy. Common Cause intends to pressure them accordingly.

In addition to knocking down these direct barriers to voting, we must also dismantle indirect ones. We must realize that solving our election crisis is not just a matter of making sure our election systems work effectively and efficiently for those who attempt to vote, but also a matter of encouraging people to turn out to vote in the first place. In each of the past two presidential elections, only about half of the voting-age population in the United States voted. Since it hit almost 47 percent in 1970, the percentage of voting-age Americans turning out for mid-term congressional elections has failed to breach 40 percent. As a result, those holding the highest federal offices in the nation are elected with support from only a fraction of American adults (in the country as a whole in the case of the President, and in states or congressional districts for Members of Congress).

This crisis of low voter turnout is rooted in complicated individual and social dynamics, but there are unnecessary institutional barriers to participation that we can eliminate. The Medill School of Journalism at Northwestern University polled nonvoters after the last election, asking them what policy changes might increase the odds that they would vote in future elections. The two policy changes cited by the highest percentage of respondents are instructive. Sixty-four percent of respondents said same-day registration would make it more likely that they would vote, and 57 percent said that expanding the voting period to two or three days would have that effect. While it would be a mistake to rush these reforms into existence without careful consideration and the necessary preparations, these poll numbers point out the need to both enhance the opportunity to vote and dismantle administrative hurdles to the ballot box.

The six states that currently have same-day registration have turnout rates significantly higher than the national average. This provides compelling evidence that we can increase turnout by preventing registration deadlines from making voters ineligible before the campaign season hits its prime in the final weeks before the election. Of course, almost every state in the union would need more sophisticated voter databases and the accompanying computer resources to institute same-day registration without exposing our elections to potential fraud and confusion. The Connecticut legislature, for example, is considering a bill to mandate that local electoral jurisdictions connect to a statewide voter database. If this effort to create a single, unified list of voters in the state prevails, Connecticut will pave the way for citizens to register and vote on the same day, while simultaneously minimizing the risk that voters would be able to fraudulently vote in multiple jurisdictions. Until we have the necessary systems and technological resources in place, however, we unfortunately will have to approach same-day voter registration with a sense of caution and experimentation.

Some have promoted the idea of taking this notion of a single unified database to its next logical conclusion. They advocate the creation of a nationwide voter database that would extend to the entire nation the advantages mentioned above with regard to the proposal in Connecticut. Others believe that such a nationwide list would jeopardize privacy and pave the way for a discriminatorily applied system of identification. While these latter concerns must be taken with the seriousness they deserve, we should consider fully any policy changes that might help ensure that registration deadlines and procedures do not deter or prevent citizens from voting, while also protecting the integrity of our elections. While Common Cause shares the reservations mentioned above and has not endorsed the development of a nationwide voter database, we think this idea should be on the table.

Like removing the logistical impediments to voting caused by certain registration rules, moving the voting period outside of the bounds of a single workday is a commonsense reform to expand the opportunity to vote. Our society, culture, and economy present many Americans with great stresses on their time as they struggle to balance the demands of employment, family, and other responsibilities. The practice of holding our elections on a regular Tuesday—generally with the polls open for only a few hours outside of regular business hours—fails to recognize the realities of our contemporary lifestyles. Voting holds a sacred place in our system of government, and it should hold a special place on our calendar.

Some have proposed moving Presidents' Day or Veterans' Day to the first Tuesday in November as a way to accomplish this goal. Others have suggested that we move our elections to a weekend or a two-or-three day period within the week. We should consider carefully the potential pros and cons of all such proposals to determine the best way to provide Americans with an expanded opportunity to vote each election year.

Voting holds a sacred place in our system of government, and it should hold a special place on our calendar.

In addition to preventing registration requirements or the narrow confines of our current election day from deterring would-be voters, we must aggressively pursue other factors and policies that might lead to increases in our unacceptably low voter turnout. Turnout rates vary significantly across our 50 states, as well as across the more than one hundred democracies around the world. This Commission and others working on this issue, like Common Cause, should conduct comparison analyses of electoral jurisdictions to identify the best practices for increasing turnout that also square with American democratic values.

I consider the reforms I have mentioned thus far to be the fundamental elements of a practical and effective election reform agenda: replacing outdated voting machines, ensuring adequate resources at all polling places, instituting error-proof voter list maintenance procedures, re-enfranchising ex-felons, greatly reducing the burdens of registration, and enhancing the opportunity to vote by changing the period over which voting is conducted. Common Cause also urges the Commission to carefully consider more sweeping changes to our election systems that could yield a more democratic political process.

We support the end of the Electoral College and the direct election of the President, although we understand that this is not a politically viable proposal at this time. Common Cause has been involved in past efforts to abolish the Electoral College, some of which garnered serious attention in Congress. Currently, some of our state organizations are working to change the typical winner-take-all systems for choosing electors, and we will continue to be active in such efforts.

Common Cause also supports Instant Run-Off Voting (IRV), and we are considering support for proportional representation voting systems. IRV is an important tool for ensuring that the will of the majority is reflected in electoral outcomes in cases when multiple candidates vie for a single seat. While it is a complicated issue that Common Cause has yet to fully and adequately explore, proportional representation voting may also lead to legislative bodies that more precisely reflect the will of the constituencies they were created to represent. Because many election districts have been drawn in an imbalanced way to protect powerful incumbents, a high percentage of American voters live in election districts that continually prevent them from voting for an ultimately victorious candidate

> ## We support the end of the Electoral College and the direct election of the President.

who shares their general political perspective. Proportional representation voting systems lead to a higher percentage of voters casting ballots for successful candidates and feeling truly represented in our legislative bodies. While remaining cognizant of potential drawbacks, we should consider the potential for this reform to inspire people to participate.

Short of proportional representation, or in addition to it, we need to change the way redistricting is done in many states, so that the process serves the interests of our democracy rather than the exclusive interests of powerful incumbents who are anxious to expand their electoral majorities. At key points in the past decades, Common Cause has worked in many states to make the redistricting process more open and inclusive of public participation—to shape the redistricting process in a way that increases the likelihood that electoral districts will be drawn with the interests of our democracy in mind, not just the interests of powerful incumbent legislators. We fully intend to continue our focus on this issue, particularly as it becomes increasingly prominent in the coming months.

Finally, we believe the Commission should also comment on one additional egregious abridgement of voting rights. While not directly denied the right to vote, the approximately 500,000 American citizens who live in the District of Columbia are effectively disenfranchised by the fact that they have only a non-voting delegate in the U.S. House and no representation at all in the U.S. Senate. In a nation with a history of consistently expanding the franchise, D.C. residents are the next set of Americans whose voting rights we must secure.

The reforms I have mentioned—both the more practical and the more sweeping—will require legislative action at the federal, state, and local level. Common Cause believes that Congress should act as soon as possible to appropriate significant funds for grants to state and local governments to implement a set of the best electoral practices that it identifies, and that strings should be attached to this federal funding to ensure that those state and local governments take baseline steps to protect voting rights. Bipartisan bills to this effect have already been introduced on Capitol Hill, and we are lobbying in support of the best of them. However, while it appears that federal financial support and guidance will be necessary to achieve

---

We must prepare to move state by state in support of policy changes that ensure that our elections more faithfully serve the principles of our democracy.

---

needed change, the heavy lifting on many of the election reforms I have mentioned today must be done at the state level. I believe it is unlikely that elections will be federalized in a wholesale fashion, and I am not convinced that it is necessary or appropriate. Therefore, we must prepare to move state by state in support of policy changes that ensure that our elections more faithfully serve the principles of our democracy. If real and meaningful reforms are to be enacted before our next elections, citizens and their organizations must mobilize around these critical issues, and place overwhelming pressure on our political leaders for change.

On behalf of Common Cause and the Common Cause Education Fund, I pledge to you that we will employ our nationwide organizational resources in support of sound recommendations that the Commission makes this fall to fix our flawed election systems and re-engage citizens in our political process. The Common Cause Education Fund will continue to do research and work to educate the public about the critical issues at stake in election reform. Common Cause—our 501c(4) lobbying arm—will continue its work to fashion a legislative reform strategy for all levels of government, and to mobilize a broad-based coalition and intense grassroots support behind that legislative strategy.

Thank you again for providing me with this opportunity to testify before you today.

Opening Statement on Campaign Finance Reform[4]

John McCain

Republican United States Senator, Arizona, 1985– ; born Panama Canal Zone, August 29, 1936; graduated United States Naval Academy, 1958; naval aviator, 1958–80; shot down over Vietnam, 1967, and held as prisoner-of-war in Hanoi, 1967–73; retired from the Navy as Captain, 1981; U.S. Representative from Arizona, 1982–85; Chairman of U.S. Senate on Commerce, Science and Transportation; military honors include Silver Star, Bronze Star, Legion of Merit, Purple Heart, and Distinguished Flying Cross; named one of the "25 Most Influential People in America" by Time, *1997; author,* Faith of My Fathers: A Family Memoir, *2000.*

Editors' introduction: To curtail what they perceived to be the dominant influence of powerful interests, in 2001, Senators John McCain, Republican from Arizona, and Russell Feingold, Democrat from Wisconsin, sponsored legislation in the U.S. Senate to ban "soft money" campaign contributions and limit political advertisements by independent groups. Opponents to the McCain-Feingold bill, led by Senator Mitch McConnell, Republican from Kentucky, maintained that soft-money contributions were a form of free political speech protected by the First Amendment. In the speech below, Senator McCain states that his "purpose" is "to enact fair, bipartisan campaign finance reform that seeks no special advantage for one party or another."

John McCain's speech: Mr. President, today we begin the first open Senate debate in many years on whether or not we should substantially reform our campaign finance laws. I want to thank Senators Lott and Daschle for their commitment to allowing a fair and open debate, and for their assurance that the Senate will be allowed to exercise its will on this matter and vote on the legislation that emerges at the end of the amendment process.

I want to thank as well, Senator McConnell, our steadfast and all-too-capable opponent, who honestly and bravely defends his beliefs, for agreeing to the terms of this debate, a debate that we hope may settle many of the questions, held by advocates and opponents of reform, that have yet to be resolved by this body.

---

4. Delivered in the United States Senate, Washington D.C., March 19, 2001.

I, of course, want to thank from the bottom of my heart, all the co-sponsors of this legislation for their steadfast support, and for proving to be far more able and persuasive advocates of our cause than I have had the skill to be.

Most particularly, I want to thank my partner in this long endeavor, Senator Russ Feingold, a man of rare courage and decency, who has risked his own career and ambitions for the sake of his principles. To me, Mr. President, that seems a pretty good definition of patriotism.

I want to thank the President of the United States for engaging in this debate, and for his oft stated willingness to seek a fair resolution of our differences on this issue for the purpose of providing the people we serve greater confidence in the integrity of their public institutions. Too often, as this debate approached, our differences on this issue have been viewed as an extension of our former rivalry. I regret that very much. For he is not my rival. He is my President, and he retains my confidence that the country we love will be a better place because of his leadership.

Lastly, Mr. President, I wish to thank every member of the Senate—especially Senator Hagel, my friend yesterday, my friend today, my friend tomorrow—for their cooperation in allowing this debate to occur so early in what will surely be one of the busier congressional sessions in recent memory. I thank all my colleagues for their patience, a patience that has been tried by my own numerous faults far too often, as I beg their indulgence again. Please accept my assurance that no matter our various differences on this issue, and my own failings in arguing those differences, my purpose is limited solely to enacting those reforms that we believe are necessary to defend the government's public trust, and not to seek a personal advantage at any colleague's expense.

I sincerely hope that our debate, contentious though it will be, will also be free of acrimony and rancor, and that the quality of our deliberations will impress the public as evidence of the good faith that sustains our resolve.

Mr. President, the many sponsors of this legislation have but one purpose: to enact fair, bipartisan campaign finance reform that seeks no special advantage for one party or another, but that helps change the public's widespread belief that politicians have no greater purpose than our own re-election. And to that end, we will respond disproportionately to the needs of those interests that can best finance our ambition, even if those interests conflict with the public interest and with the governing philosophy we once sought office to advance.

The sad truth is, Mr. President, that most Americans do believe that we conspire to hold onto every single political advantage we have, lest we jeopardize our incumbency by a single lost vote. Most Americans believe that we would let this nation pay any price, bear any burden for the sake of securing our own ambitions, no matter how injurious the effect might be to the national interest. And who can blame them. As long as the wealthiest Americans and richest organized interests can make the six and seven figure donations to political parties and gain the special access to power that such generosity confers on the donor, most Americans will dismiss the most virtuous politician's claim of patriotism.

> *Public opinion polls consistently show that the vast majorities of our constituents want reform.*

The opponents of reform will ask if the public so distrusts us and so dislikes our current campaign finance system why is there no great cry in the country to throw us all out of office? They will contend—and this point is disputable—that no one has ever lost or won an election because of their opposition to or support for campaign finance reform. Yet public opinion polls consistently show that the vast majorities of our constituents want reform, and believe our current system of campaign financing is terribly harmful to the public good. But, the opponents observe, they do not rank reform among the national priorities they expect their government to urgently address. That is true, Mr. President, but why is it so?

Simply put, they don't believe it will ever be done. They don't expect us to adopt real reforms and they defensively keep their hopes from being raised and their inevitable disappointment from being worse.

The public just doesn't believe that either an incumbent opposing reform or a challenger supporting it will honestly work to repair this system once he or she has been elected under the rules, or lack thereof, that govern it. They distrust both. They believe that whether we publicly advocate or oppose reform, we are all working either openly or deceitfully to prevent even the slightest repair of a system they believe is corrupt.

So they avoid investing too much hope in the possibility that we could surprise them. And they accommodate their disappointment by basing their pride in their country on their own patriotism and that of their neighbors, on the civilization they have built and defended, and not on the hope that politicians will ever take courage from our convictions and not our campaign treasuries.

Our former colleague, Senator David Boren of Oklahoma, recently reminded me of a poll that *Time* magazine has conducted over many years. In 1961, 76% Americans said yes to the question, "Do you trust your government to do the right thing?" This year, only 19% of Americans still believed that. Many events have occurred in the last thirty years to fuel their distrust, Mr. President. Assassinations, Vietnam, Watergate, and many subsequent public scandals have squandered the public's faith in us, and have led more and more Americans from even taking responsibility for our election. But surely frequent campaign finance scandals and their real or assumed connection to misfeasance by public officials are a major part of the problem.

Why should they not be? Any voter with a healthy understanding of the flaws of human nature and who notices the vast amounts of money solicited and received by politicians cannot help but believe that we are unduly influenced by our benefactors' generosity.

Why can't we all agree to this very simple, very obvious truth: that campaign contributions from a single source that run to the hundreds of thousands or millions of dollars are not healthy to a democracy? Is that not self-evident? It is to the people, Mr. President. It is to the people.

Some will argue that there isn't too much money in politics. They will argue there's not enough. They will argue that soft money, the huge, unregulated revenue stream into political party coffers, is necessary to ensure the strength of the two party system. I find this last point hard to understand considering that in the fifteen years or so that soft money has become the dominant force in our elections the parties have grown appreciably weaker as independents become the fastest growing voter registration group in the country.

Some will observe that we spend more money to advertise toothpaste and yogurt in this country than to conduct campaigns for public office. I don't care, Mr. President. I'm not concerned with the costs of toothpaste and yogurt. We aren't selling those commodities to the public. We are offering our integrity and our principles, and the means we use to market them should not cause the consumer to doubt the value of the product.

Some will argue that the First Amendment of the Constitution renders unlawful any restrictions on the right of anyone to raise unlimited amounts of money for political campaigns. Mr. President, which drafter of the Constitution believed or anticipated that the First Amendment would be exercised in political campaigns by the relatively few at the expense of the many?

We have restrictions now that have been upheld by the courts; they have simply been circumvented by the rather recent exploitation of the so-called soft money loophole. Teddy Roosevelt signed a law banning corporate contributions. Harry Truman signed a law banning contributions from labor unions. In 1974, we enacted a law to limit contributions by individuals and political action committees directly to the candidates. Those laws were not found unconstitutional and vacated by the courts. They were judged lawful for the purpose of preventing political corruption or the appearance of corruption.

Those laws were rendered ineffectual not unlawful by the ingenuity of politicians determined to get around them who used an allowance in the law that placed no restrictions on what once was intended essentially to be a building fund for the state parties. Now, Mr. President, that fund has run to the billions of dollars, and I haven't noticed the buildings that serve as our local and state party headquarters becoming quite that magnificent.

Ah, say the opponents, if politicians will always find a way of circumventing campaign finance laws, what's the point of passing new laws? Do I believe that any law will prove effective over time? No, I do not. Were we to pass this legislation today, I am sure that at some time in the future, hopefully many years from now, we will need to address some new circumvention. So what. So we have to debate this matter again. Is that such a burden on us or our successors that we should simply be indifferent to the abundant evidence of at least the appearance of corruption and to the public's ever growing alienation from the government of this great nation, problems that this system has engendered? I hope not, Mr. President, I hope not.

Mr. President, the supporters of this legislation have had differences about what constitutes the ideal reform, but we have subordinated those differences to the common good, in the hope that we might enact those basic reforms that members of both parties could agree on. It is not perfect reform. There is no perfect reform. It could be improved and we hope it will be during this debate. We have tried to exclude any provision that could be viewed as placing one party or the other at a disadvantage. Our intention is to pass the best, most balanced, most important reforms we can. All we ask of our colleagues is that they approach this debate with the same purpose in mind.

I beg my colleagues not to propose amendments intended only to kill this legislation or to seize on any change in this legislation that serves our basic goal as an excuse to withdraw your support. The sponsors want to have votes on all relevant issues involved in campaign finance reform and will support amendments that strengthen the bipartisan majority in favor of reform and that do not prevent us from achieving our fundamental goal of substantially reducing the influence of big money on our political system.

If we cannot agree on every aspect of reform; if we have differences about what constitutes genuine and necessary reform, and we hold those differences honestly—so be it. Let us try to come to terms with those differences fairly. That is what the sponsors of this legislation have tried to do, and we welcome anyone's help to improve upon our efforts as long as that help is sincere and intended to reach the common goal of genuine campaign finance reform.

Mr. President, I hope we will, for the moment, forget our partisan imperatives and take a risk for our country. Perhaps that is a hopelessly naïve aspiration. It need not be. I think the good men and women I am privileged to serve with are perfectly capable of surprising a skeptical public, and maybe ourselves, by taking on this challenge to the honor of the profession of which we are willing and proud members.

Real campaign finance reform will not cure all public cynicism about modern politics. Nor will it completely free politics from influence peddling or the appearance of it. But I believe it will cause many Americans who are at present quite disaffected from the machinations of politics to begin to see that their elected officials value their reputations more than their incumbency. And maybe that recognition will cause them to exercise their franchise more faithfully, to identify more closely with political parties, to raise their expectations for the work we do. Maybe it will even encourage more of them to seek public office, not for the privileges bestowed upon election winners, but for the honor of serving a great nation.

Thank you, Mr. President.

Proposing an Amendment to the Constitution of the United States[5]

Mitch McConnell

Republican United States Senator from Kentucky, 1985– ; born Tuscumbia, AL, February 20, 1942, and raised in South Louisville, KY; attended Louisville, KY public schools; B.A. with honors, University of Louisville, 1964; graduated University of Kentucky Law School, 1967; legislative assistant to Senator Marlow Cook, 1968–70; deputy assistant United States Attorney, 1974–75; elected judge-executive of Jefferson County, KY, 1978–85; chairman, Select Committee on Ethics, U.S. Senate, 1995–97; ranking Republican U.S. Senate Rules Committee, with jurisdiction over federal election law; ranking member Foreign Operations Appropriations Subcommittee; senior member, Agriculture and Appropriations Committees; named by the Congressional Quarterly *and* George *magazine as one of Washington's most powerful people.*

Editors' introduction: In the Senate, John McCain, Republican from Arizona, and Russell Feingold, Democrat from Wisconsin, sponsored legislation to ban "soft money" campaign contributions and limit political advertisements by independent groups. In leading the opposition to the McCain-Feingold bill, and to friendly amendments attached to it, Senator Mitch McConnell insisted that "to do what McCain Feingold's proponents want to do—restrict all spending by, in support of and in opposition to candidates—then you need to get rid of the first amendment."

Mitch McConnell's speech: Madam President, the proposal of the Senator from South Carolina to eviscerate the first amendment is as refreshing as it is frightful.

It is a blunt instrument, this proposed amendment to the Constitution. It consists of a simple paragraph repeated twice so that the State governments, as well as Congress, would be empowered to restrict the heretofore sacrosanct, all contributions and spending "by, in support of, or in opposition to candidates for public office."

The whole political ballgame: citizen groups, individuals, parties and the candidates.

Unlike the McCain-Feingold, the [Senator Ernest] Hollings constitutional amendment does not include a special exemption for the news and entertainment media.

---

5. Delivered in the United States Senate on March 26, 2001.

And unlike the McCain-Feingold debate, the casual observer will not be confused by the campaign finance vocabulary. "Issue advocacy," "express advocacy," "electioneering," "soft money," "hard money"—these terms of art in the McCain-Feingold debate are absent from the Hollings constitutional amendment, which reads simply: "by, in support of, or in opposition to."

Plain English. These eight words in the Hollings constitutional amendment sum up the reformers' agenda for the past quarter-century as they have sought to root out of American political life any speech or activity which could conceivably affect an election or be of value to a politician.

Except the media's speech, of course. McCain-Feingold takes care of them with a special exemption on page 15 of their bill to foreclose prosecution of their "electioneering" in newspapers, on radio and television.

The Hollings amendment reaches right in and rips the heart right out of the First Amendment.

No pretense. No artifice. No question about it. If you believe that the government—federal and state—ought to be omnipotent in their power to restrict all contributions and spending "by, in support of, or in opposition to" candidates for public office, then the Hollings amendment is for you.

If you believe that the United States Supreme Court should be taken out of the campaign finance equation, then the Hollings constitutional amendment is for you.

If the Hollings amendment had been in place twenty-five years ago, there would have been no *Buckley v. Valeo* decision. Congress would have gotten its way in the 1970s: independent expenditures would be capped at $1,000. Any issue advocacy that FEC bureaucrats deem capable of influencing an election would be capped at $1,000.

Citizen groups would have to disclose to the government their donor lists. Sierra Club members who live in small towns out west where environmentalists are not universally revered—and whose need for anonymity has been cited by Sierra Club officials as the reason they keep donor names secret—would have their names publicly listed on a government database, probably the Internet.

All of us politicians' campaigns would be constrained by mandatory spending limits. There would be no "millionaire's loophole" because millionaires would be under the spending limits, too.

There would be no taxpayer financing. It would not be necessary, because spending limits would not have to be voluntary.

That's why the American Civil Liberties Union counsel, Joel Gora, who was part of the legal team in the *Buckley* case has labeled the Hollings constitutional amendment: a "recipe for repression."

The media—news and entertainment divisions—ought to take note. There is no exemption for them in the Hollings constitutional amendment. No media "loophole." Under the Hollings constitutional amendment, the federal and state governments could regulate, restrict, even prohibit, the media's own issue advocacy, independent expenditures and contributions. Just so long as the restrictions were deemed "reasonable."

I commend the Senator from South Carolina for offering this amendment, insofar as he lays out on the table just what the stakes are in the campaign finance debate.

To do what the reformers say they want to do—limit "special interest" influence—requires limiting the United States Constitution which gives "special interest"—that is, all Americans—the freedom to speak, the freedom to associate with others in a cause, and the freedom to petition the government for a redress of grievances.

You have to gut the first amendment. You have to throw out on the trash heap that freedom which the U.S. Supreme Court said six decades ago, is "the matrix, the indispensable condition of nearly every other form of freedom."

If you believe McCain-Feingold is constitutional, as its advocates claim it is, then you do not need the Hollings constitutional amendment. In fact, Senator Feingold is against the constitutional amendment.

If you vote for the Hollings constitutional amendment, then you have affirmed what so many of us in and outside of the Senate have been saying: that to do what McCain-Feingold's proponents want to do—restrict all spending by, in support of and in opposition to candidates—then you need to get rid of the first amendment. That is the core of the problem.

If you really want to reduce special interest influence on American politics, you need to get rid of the first amendment.

Fortunately, Madam President, this amendment, which Senator Hollings has certainly persevered in offering over the years, continues to lose support. The first time I was involved in this debate back in 1988, it actually passed—bearing in mind it requires 67, a majority, for this amendment— 52-42. That rough majority persisted in a second vote in 1988 and then a sense of the Senate vote in 1993.

Then in 1995 the support for it dropped from 52 down to 45 and in 1997 from 45 down to 38, and last year, March 28, 2000, this proposal was defeated 67-33. Only 33 Senators a year ago believed it was appropriate to amend the Constitution for the first time in history to give the Government this kind of power.

One of the reasons this constitutional amendment is growing in unpopularity is that it has a lot of opponents. Common Cause is opposed to it. I ask unanimous consent two letters from Common Cause on the subject be printed in the *[Congressional] Record.* . . .

III. Education

Education Is Everybody's Business[1]

Liam E. McGee

President, Bank of America California, 2000– ; a native of Ireland, has lived in California nearly all of his life; speaks Spanish fluently; bachelor's degree in business administration, University of San Diego; M.B.A., Pepperdine University; law degree, Loyola Law School; head of Bank of America California consumer bank, 1990–95; head of Bank of America California technology and operations group, 1996–98; president, Bank of America, Southern California, 1998–2000; Group Executive Vice President for Bank of America's National Consumer Support Services; member, Operating Committee of Bank of America; member, boards of San Francisco Museum of Modern Art and the Autry Museum of Western Heritage; two-term member, Federal Reserve Bank of San Francisco board of directors; chairman, United Way of Greater Los Angeles; chairman, board of trustees University of San Diego; member, board of Anderson School UCLA.

Editors' introduction: Liam E. McGee addressed the Town Hall of Los Angeles at the Omni Hotel. He spoke to about 250 Town Hall members, foundation representatives, educators, and business leaders. The speech was audiotaped and sent to radio stations for replay. President McGee advised that education is "the biggest challenge facing our nation and our society."

Liam E. McGee's speech: Today, I'd like to discuss the most important challenge facing the banking industry in the new millennium. No, I'm not going to deliver a rousing address on electronic commerce, interest rate sensitivity, loan securitization or ATM access fees!

Instead, I'd like to talk about education. It's the most important issue facing banking or any other industry. As a matter of fact, it's the biggest challenge facing our nation and our society.

Now having just finished a nice lunch you may be thinking, oh no, not another oratorical lament about the dismal plight of our public schools! You've probably heard as many of them as I have. Each one seems filled with the same stale clichés and shopworn platitudes.

---

1. Delivered in Los Angeles, California, on June 14, 2000, at a noon lunch. Reprinted with permission of Liam E. McGee.

While I can't promise a speech completely devoid of familiar topics, what I hope to do is stimulate your thinking and spark some discussion by focusing on three themes:

First, the new economy demands employees who are literate and creative, willing to learn and able to adapt. For the most part, our public schools are failing to produce those employees. Southern California's economic prosperity and America's global competitiveness will be at risk until we change that.

Second, the business community must do more than just complain about schools, we must offer constructive reform ideas and strong community leadership to make change happen. By applying some key business principles to our public schools, we can make that needed contribution.

And third, I'll conclude by suggesting that no community anywhere in the world has a better opportunity—or a more compelling need—to lead on school reform than Los Angeles.

I've had some experience in education reform in Southern California on the LAAMP/LEARN and Junior Achievement boards, among others, as well as serving as a volunteer teacher. And, I've recently invested a lot of personal time in fiscal reform work with LAUSD.

So, I know there isn't an easy fix to addressing the education needs in our state, but we have the chance of a lifetime, and we can't afford to pass it up.

The New Economy and the Link to Schools

Over the last two decades, we've elected education presidents, education governors, education congressmen and education state legislators. It seems like we'll vote for anyone who says they'll make schools the top priority.

But did you notice what happened when hundreds of billions of dollars in budget surpluses materialized in Washington, D.C.?

What was the rally cry that went forth from the corridors of the White House and the halls of Congress? Was it "Save Our Schools First?" No. It was—and is "Save Social Security First."

A cynical person might suggest it's because the kids can't vote and the seniors do. But the irony is that in the long run the only viable way to preserve the social safety net for seniors is to dramatically improve the public education for children. Let me explain the link.

America is aging and it is having fewer children. Over the next 30 years, the 65-and-over population will double, from 35 million today to 70 million. The ratio of workers to retirees will continue to shrink. In 1950 there were 16 workers for each Social Security beneficiary. Today that ratio is just three to one. By the year 2030, there will be only two workers for each retiree.

The point is this: Tomorrow's smaller workforce must be better educated and more productive in order to support the exploding senior population.

In addition, our high-tech, information-driven, service-oriented economy is demanding that each of these scarce workers be equipped with the skills and creativity to function in a constantly changing and fiercely competitive economic environment. Unfortunately, economic and technological advances have outpaced educational achievement.

Public schools here in Los Angeles and across the nation are not producing the graduates we must have for continued advances in productivity and prosperity, and many companies are finding it difficult to find qualified workers.

Tomorrow's smaller workforce must be better educated and more productive in order to support the exploding senior population.

A few years ago at the Bank of America, 40 percent of entry-level job applicants failed an employment test written at the seventh-grade level. And we were not alone. Other companies have reported failure rates even higher.

My friends, we're producing kids who aren't ready for the global economy. Children in Japan and Germany attend school an average of 240 days a year, compared to 180 days here. Over a young person's K-12 school career, that amounts to three years of additional class time.

Instead we're lucky if our graduates even know how to read. Across the nation an estimated 700,000 graduates are unable to read their diplomas. And in many urban areas, the high school dropout rate exceeds 50 percent.

Here in California, some 80 percent of fourth-grade school children don't read as well as they should. That's a terribly frightening statistic because the evidence is clear: Children who don't read by age nine very often fail to catch up.

A *Los Angeles Times* poll conducted in April found that education was the number-one concern of Angelenos—ahead of crime, even ahead of traffic.

Seventy percent of the parents with students in the public schools rated those schools poor to fair. There's plenty of evidence to back up their perception. California's new Academic Performance Index rated 541 Los Angeles public schools. Only 21 elementary schools attained the state's target score of 800. And not one secondary school hit the mark.

Make no mistake. You and I pay a staggering price for failing to adequately train our young people for productive lives. It's a cost we can't afford.

I'd go even further to suggest that the failure to revitalize our K–12 schools poses the single greatest threat to our long-term prosperity here and across the nation. I think you can see why education is indeed everybody's business.

Applying Business Principles to Public Schools

That brings me to my second theme. Business must do more than just complain about public schools. We must bring creative ideas and strong leadership to the reform effort. This has already started to happen. In fact, the *Los Angeles Times* has observed that Wall Street sees education as the next industry ripe for growth and restructuring.

With the impact of the Internet, advances in technology and greater interest from the private sector, education reform is sweeping the country. Not only are educators and parents weighing in, business leaders are becoming increasingly involved.

Thanks to all of these concerned voices, I'm encouraged that some of the hardened interest group positions in the school reform debate are starting to soften. Consensus is emerging. After nearly two decades of big talk and little action, change is starting to happen.

On the national level we see both major party presidential candidates bringing substance and a measure of fresh thinking to the education debate. Both seem to be moving their parties away from previously hardened positions.

Governor Bush has made it clear that school quality is indeed worthy of strong national leadership and appropriate federal involvement. Vice President Gore told his allies in the teachers unions that there *must* be a clear link between salary increases and better student performance.

In Sacramento, Governor Davis and the legislature have significantly boosted education funding. The gap between what California spends per student and what the nation as a whole spends has been closed, at least for this year. This funding has come with stringent performance and accountability standards attached.

Frankly, I don't know that you can call education a business or even run it like one, but I do believe there are some basic business principles that can be applied to the classroom.

First, strengthen leadership at the top.

We should empower our principals as leaders and managers. If they deliver, they ought to control budgets, personnel decisions, changes in curriculum and school schedules.

I think Governor Tom Carper of Delaware summed it up best when he said, "I've never been to a great school where they don't have a great principal.

Not only do we need strong leaders; we have to get smarter about how our schools are being run.

> *Not only do we need strong leaders; we have to get smarter about how our schools are being run.*

The average elementary school in Los Angeles has approximately 1,000 students. To me, that qualifies as a pretty big business. As leaders of these businesses, our principals should have the authority and accountability to manage their teams and appoint their department heads.

We should ensure that our schools have access to technology and management information systems, so principals and teachers have the tools they need to manage at a local level.

Many school districts are in the business of buying real estate, running warehouses, staffing janitorial functions and handling bus schedules. Schools should be outsourcing to people who can do them cheaper and better. Our educators' time should be spent where it counts—teaching our kids—not negotiating real estate deals or buying supplies.

Successful business organizations encourage decentralization. They push resources, information and decision-making authority away from headquarters, toward district offices that are nearer the customers.

Our school systems should do the same. Thanks to our departing interim superintendent, Ramon Cortines, the L.A. Unified School District has taken a step in the right direction.

His plan to reduce the district's huge central bureaucracy and create 11 smaller subdistricts—and more recently to advance pay-for-performance ideas—represents the kind of creative management that our schools desperately need.

Still, we've got a long way to go. Unfortunately, but perhaps understandably, our society is not adequately preparing educators to become leaders. That's got to change.

Unless educators learn to run the large and complex public schools establishment, reform will produce little in the way of progress.

Organizations like the Broad Foundation have committed substantial funding to the development of school leaders. It has announced a $100 million initiative to improve leadership, governance and management in large urban districts.

Other organizations are promoting similar efforts. The University of California at Riverside, for example, has undertaken a leadership development program with $1 million from Bank of America.

Once they're equipped with the proper skills and empowered with the authority to make decisions, principals must be held fully accountable for their performance. Excellent leaders must be recognized and rewarded; those who fall short must be retrained or removed, which leads me to my second business principle:

Encourage competition

We need to bring competition in from the playing field and reintroduce it in the classroom. This concept isn't new, but has been slow to take root.

The National Alliance of Business recently reported that while the private sector encourages hard work, innovation and high standards through the risks and rewards of competition, public schools, educators and students have faced few consequences for their failures and even fewer for their successes.

There's no doubt that greater accountability is necessary if schools are going to compete more effectively. Public schools no longer have a monopoly on education, and to survive, they must be able to compete.

The fact is, worthy competitors already exist. And, parents have more options than ever when considering what schools their children should attend.

Last month, the Kansas City school district became the first urban district to lose its accredited status for failing all of Missouri's performance standards. Unless there is a turnaround, the district could be abolished.

There's no doubt—Choice and competition are on the rise.

For example, consider the nationwide charter school movement. There are now some 1,200 of these schools in 36 states, including California, schools that provide parents with a measure of choice and schools administrators with a badly needed dose of competition, without undermining the concept of public education.

Education is now a $600 billion industry. Some people think it will become the next growth industry of the 21st century. And I have to think that enterprising business leaders will find ways to train students better, faster and less expensively than the current system.

Plenty of experiments are underway. Here in Los Angeles, several years ago, financier Michael Milkin introduced his Knowledge Universe. Entrepreneur Chris Whittle founded the Edison Project, which provides an alternative to public school management. And New York philanthropist Ted Forstmann drew attention by making private vouchers available to a number of underprivileged children.

To many people, vouchers are an anathema. Mention the idea to public educators, and they're likely to react like the wicked witch come into contact with water.

But like it or not, the nationwide voucher movement is a wake-up call to educators everywhere—an unambiguous expression of the mounting dissatisfaction with our current system.

Unless our teachers and administrators preserve public education by taking it forward, unless they dramatically improve our schools by embracing tough standards and strict accountability, parents and taxpayers will abandon today's system for the expanding array of privately sponsored alternatives.

The challenge is clear and immediate!

And, while we're talking about competition, let's talk a bit about compensation. My final business principle is:

Ensure market-based compensation

The teacher in the classroom is the single most important factor in raising the academic performance of our students, bar none.

We put our children in their hands every day, and yet there are teachers who struggle to make ends meet.

We talk about what a noble profession teaching is. But, we wouldn't have to rely on the nobility of teaching to attract quality people if we did a better job of treating them as professionals.

But, the point is not simply to treat all current teachers better to show our appreciation.

The point is to raise standards, compensation and prestige so that our best and brightest kids choose to enter the teaching profession, and the best teachers should be recognized publicly for their great work just like the best doctors, lawyers and business leaders.

Those who fail to perform should be retrained or removed. Failing to do so demoralizes the excellent teachers we already have and cripples our ability to attract the best and the brightest young people to the profession.

Due to retirements and increasing enrollments, our nation is going to need two million new teachers over the next decade. We'll need 300,000 in California alone.

If we want good teachers, we must pay them a decent salary. That means paying educators according to their worth—not how long they've been there.

I was encouraged when the nation's second largest teachers' union, the Federation of American Teachers, signaled its willingness to accept tougher standards for the teaching profession.

Merit pay for teachers is clearly an idea whose time has come.

But the reality is that the education establishment, especially the teachers' unions, must go further. They need to recognize that a funding and pay system based solely on student population and teacher seniority—instead of results—will only breed complacency and mediocrity.

And this, in turn, will undermine support for public education. Merit pay for teachers is clearly an idea whose time has come. Ideas like scholarships in exchange for teaching commitments, signing bonuses, and higher pay for improved student performance are all catching on, as they must.

With a little imagination, all of us can help. At Bank of America we've created the Teacher Flex Mortgage program that enables teachers to buy homes with little or nothing down.

The philosophy behind this program is simple. Those who are devoting their lives to teaching our children ought to be able to share in the American dream of owning a home.

I'm sure you've heard about Governor Davis' recent proposal to exempt teachers from the California state income tax. He's received a lot of criticism for the idea. I, for one, might look upon it more favorably if the Governor would include in the exemption those of us struggling for survival in the banking industry!

But seriously, I applaud the governor for his out-of-the-box thinking. We must consider bold, innovative, even unorthodox approaches to address the shortage of teachers and upgrade the quality of the profession.

I agree with IBM chairman and CEO Lou Gerstner who in a speech to the National Education Summit in New York clearly identified the one thing standing between students and stronger performance.

He said, "High student achievement is possible. But it will only follow high teacher achievement."

A Leadership Opportunity for Los Angeles

Let me conclude by suggesting that here in Los Angeles, we have a unique opportunity to create a new model of excellence in our public schools. I know we can do it in our schools because we have just done it in our economy.

The 1990s began with a tremendous recession. Before it was over we had surrendered about 500,000 jobs. Plenty of people throughout our region thought we were finished.

But while the experts were biting their nails, Southern Californians were building a new economic order for the 21st century. Nearly one million entrepreneurs and small businesses—industrial companies, garments manufacturers, entertainment contractors, technology firms and dot.coms, international traders and many others—have led a powerful resurgence.

These small firms have replaced many of the big corporations that were lost during the recession. And our economy is healthier and more varied as a result.

Look at how far we've come. The Southland has 250,000 more jobs than when the recession began. Unemployment is lower than it's been in more than two decades. Wages are rising. Real estate values are up—way up. We have become the nation's premier hub for global commerce, with two-way trade through our ports expected to reach $214 billion this year.

If the five-county LA region were a separate country, we'd have the 11th largest economy in the world. But even more striking than our economy's size or strength is its diversity.

Southern California is the most ethnically diverse place in the history of the world.

More than 100 languages are spoken here in Southern California, which is home to more minority-owned businesses than any metropolitan region in the nation. Economic diversity has given rise to emerging markets throughout our region. And anyone who overlooks them won't be doing business very long.

Now, some people believe that the dispersal of Southern California's economic activity has created a leadership vacuum.

It's true that fewer large corporations are headquartered here. Many of the corporate statesmen who used to speak on behalf of the local business community and try to bring business solutions to social problems have retired. Globalization and urban sprawl have weakened civic loyalty.

What's missing, say the critics, from Los Angeles and other emerging regional economies, is the kind of corporate leadership and unified, top-down civic leadership that can be found in more traditional urban economies. These critics are not entirely wrong in their analysis, but let me make a few observations.

First, Los Angeles hardly suffers from a lack of civic leadership.

Just take a look around at the new and emerging developments that point to our city's renaissance—the world-renowned J. Paul Getty Center in Brentwood, the tremendously popular California

Science Center that is breathing new life into Exposition Park, the emerging downtown cathedral and the Walt Disney Concert Hall, which will be completed next year.

Look also at Staples Center, the site of this year's Democratic convention and home to the World Champion Los Angeles Lakers! None of these spectacular developments would have taken shape without the pride, energy and determination of our business leaders.

The current leadership has taken us far. Los Angeles is on a roll. But at the same time, a new broader system of leadership—one that truly reflects Southern California's diversity and economic decentralization—is starting to take hold.

Leadership here in the Southland is no longer the prerogative of a few Fortune 500 CEOs. The new leadership is ethnically diverse and includes community, business, labor, political and non-profit leaders, just to name a few.

And, it is a responsibility that all of us share, and it affords us an opportunity to bring creative approaches to society's most important challenges in a united rather than a divided fashion.

Challenge number-one is to revitalize our public schools. To that end, I congratulate the Los Angeles Board of Education for selecting Roy Romer to serve as our new superintendent.

Roy will bring to this position an extraordinary combination of knowledge, imagination and leadership. We're fortunate to have attracted someone so capable. Now let's all get behind him.

I see education reform as the next great touchstone of civic and business leadership, the cause and focal point around which all of us must rally.

Think about it: In a region defined by size and sprawl, diversity and decentralization, the classroom is perhaps the only place where all of us can come together and forge a real community.

As business and community leaders, parents and concerned Angelenos, we have the ability to make a real difference in our public schools. You talk to any parent; it isn't all about giving money. It's about investing the time and energy to make our schools better.

Whether it's businesses "adopting a school," employees volunteering time to tutor students, parents attending PTA meetings or simply sharing a special expertise, such as strong management skills. We can all help.

For example, at my company, we encourage our associates to volunteer two hours of paid time a week in our schools.

Working together as a community, we can transform our schools—like we transformed our economy. If you think about it, do we really have any other choice?

Ninety percent of all students in the L.A. Unified School District are ethnic minorities. For many of them, education represents an escape route from poverty, the one and only road to a better life.

Eli Broad has pointed out that our economy is becoming defined by two separate and unequal groups—service workers who struggle for $6 to $12 an hour, and knowledge workers who command far more.

Should we be content with such a society? Will we permit our public schools here in Los Angeles to become little more than day-care facilities for the service workers of the future?

No, this is a prospect that I'm unwilling to accept.

Throughout this nation's history, wave after wave of immigrants has found in education a singular opportunity to excel, to dream, to contribute.

I know, because I am one of them.

And with each succeeding generation, America has grown stronger. How many times must we relearn this same lesson? Energizing public education with greater choice and competition, stronger leadership and well-trained, better-paid teachers who embrace tough standards are not new concepts.

What is new is that we are finally starting to replace talk with action. At long last, I'm hopeful that this nation is ready to address the most dangerous threat to our economic future. It presents the greatest opportunity we have ever had to build an even stronger prosperity that this time leaves no one behind.

Thank you very much.

Educating America

A National Challenge for the 21st Century[2]

Richard A. Gephardt

Democratic Leader, House of Representatives, 1994– ; born in St. Louis, MO, January 31, 1941; B.S. Northwestern University, 1962; JD.U. University of Michigan Law School, 1965; twice elected Alderman, St. Louis's 14th Ward, 1968–71 and 1971–76; elected to represent Missouri's Third Congressional District, 1979– ; Chairman, House Democratic Caucus, 1984; Democratic candidate for president of the United States, 1988; Majority Leader, House of Representatives, 1988-94; author of An Even Better Place: America in the 21st Century, *1999.*

Editors' introduction: House Democratic Leader Richard A. Gephardt gave a special address to some 200 students, teachers, and administrators at American University, where he articulated his party's principles on educating America in the 21st century. Concerned that some American children are "not getting the time and attention they need from their parents" and that the "public schools are not now equipped to fill the breach," Mr. Gephardt insisted that "the government must help give communities the resources they need to improve their local schools." The speech was broadcast by C-SPAN.

Richard A. Gephardt's speech: Thank you, Dean Broadnax, for that generous introduction.

I am delighted to be at American University to talk about what I believe is one of the greatest issues of the 21st century, the issue of educating America.

In recent years, our nation has undergone a powerful revolution that has altered the basic contours of our social fabric. We are facing what I think of as the double challenge in contemporary American life, the challenge of child-raising and the challenge of education in the Information Age. The challenges are interconnected, and our failure to face them sows difficult, sometimes bitter seeds in our culture and our country.

Let me start by talking about the challenge of child-raising.

---

2. Delivered in Washington, D.C., on October 4, 2000, at 10:30 a.m. Reprinted with permission of Richard A. Gephardt.

For many years now, America has faced a crisis of family—a quiet crisis, but one with profound implications for our children and our future. We have undergone one of the greatest social changes since the industrial revolution, but we as a society are still in a state of denial.

The crisis has its roots in the daily struggle to balance the demands of earning a living and raising a child, at a time when most parents work outside the home, at a point when schools and other community networks are

The bottom line is children are not getting the time and attention they need from their parents.

stretched to the breaking point. This crisis can best be seen in the following, simple statistic: today, parents spend about 22 hours a week less time with their children.

The causes of this phenomenon are not hard to understand.

In recent years, the number of married mothers working for pay has increased 79%.

In the past 3 decades, the time married mothers have spent working for pay has almost doubled.

Over the same time, for two parent families, annual hours of paid work has increased 18%.

Thirty percent of all families are headed by a single parent.

Sixty percent of mothers in the workforce have children under age 6, and 75% have children between the ages of 6 and 17.

We are also spending much more time on the road, going to and from work; between 1983 and 1995, the time spent commuting to work increased 13%, and, even when families are home, they face more distractions in the form of more pagers, more phones, more television, more Internet use, and that time translates into less time together for parents and children.

The bottom line is children are not getting the time and attention they need from their parents.

And our public schools are not now equipped to fill the breach.

Instead of keeping pace with modern society, many schools are trailing behind. Instead of moving into the 21st century, many are stuck in a 1950s world of crowded classrooms, old buildings, and electrical systems that can't accommodate computers. Paint is chipping off walls, plaster, falling from ceilings, desks are too small, playgrounds, in disrepair. And there's also a national teacher shortage.

By 2009, according to the National Center for Education Statistics, America will require 2.7 million new, fully-qualified teachers to replace retiring teachers and to cope with a huge number of new students. The shortage is also the result of the large number of teachers who quit within their first five years. Approximately 30% of new teachers are quitting within five years of their hire date, and in cities, the number is even higher, almost 50%.

And who can blame them?

Some are emotionally and physically exhausted, others are required to teach in subject areas they know little about, and many are in schools where the resources and training are inadequate, and in too many of those schools there are gangs and guns instead of safety and security.

The challenge I just described has put terrible holes through America's social fabric. And our failure as a society to acknowledge that challenge has only made things worse. We have failed to fully understand that our families have changed dramatically and that there are major new demands on our public schools, and we as a people have incurred incredible costs as a result.

Children are being neglected, and *they can not raise themselves.* We know that for a fact. We know that without adequate time and attention from adults, they suffer emotionally and physically. They get into trouble, sometimes turning to drugs and violence, and they do not become productive, functional citizens. They do not fulfill their human potential.

The results of this suffering are all around us, and they are among the most painful, horrible things in America.

Every day in America, 13 children are murdered.

Every day in America, almost 300 children carry a weapon to school.

According to recent data from the Department of Education, more than 6,000 students were expelled for bringing guns or explosives to school in a single school year.

Two thirds of prison inmates are high school dropouts.

Over 2 million people in our country are in jail.

They don't pay taxes—they don't raise families—they don't contribute to charity. They are not functional citizens.

At the same time we cannot fill over 2 million job opportunities in our country.

I believe with all my heart that America can and must do better.

But how? How do we address one of the largest, most difficult issues we know? How do we give children the time and attention they need and move everyone forward into the 21st century?

The answer, I believe, lies in our public schools.

America's public schools are the only institutions with the scale and capacity to serve as the focal point for giving all children the time and attention they need and deserve.

They are the only institutions with the scale and capacity to help all children become decent, functional, productive human beings.

They can lead children toward the power of human respect, tolerance, and understanding in a world where there is still too much crime and not enough solutions.

They can help children smash through the brick walls of racism and prejudice in a country where there is still too much hate and not enough humanity.

They can help families tackle the problems of gun violence, drugs, gangs and bad neighborhoods.

And they can move every child forward into the Information Age.

This last point is essential, and it brings me to the second challenge, the challenge of educating children in the Information Age.

We live in a world defined by digital 1s and 0s and high-speed Internet connections that carry huge chunks of data around the world at the speed of light. To make your way in that world, literacy, training, knowledge and skills are absolutely essential.

Fifty years ago, education was not the key to good jobs that it is today.

In 1950, 59% of all 17-year-olds in America graduated from high school, and it was an acceptable graduation rate. You didn't need a diploma to succeed in an industrial, manufacturing economy. My father, for instance, could find a job and make a good living as a milk truck driver even though he never finished high school, and millions of Americans could do the same.

Our challenge is to tap America's bottomless capacity for innovation and hard work to lift up every school in America.

But that dynamic has changed radically. Today, public schools are the single greatest gateway to good jobs in the New Economy, and right now, we are not giving children the skills they need to succeed. This year, 70% of all 17-year-olds finished high school, and that number is too low for a hi-tech, information economy. It is not good enough for our children and it's not good enough for American businesses, which need human talent to keep their companies and the economy growing.

The subject of my talk today is public elementary and secondary education. But let me also say that every young person who wants to go to college should have that opportunity, whatever their family's income. No one should be denied a college diploma just because financial assistance is not available.

But the challenge before us today is to figure out how to marshal our national resources and collective will to give children the time and attention they are not now getting in their formative years.

I believe that the only way to do right by our children is to revolutionize every single public school in America. The simple fact is, we must have scale.

How do we achieve it?

I believe that the federal government has an important role to play by filling the holes in our social fabric that communities can't fill by themselves. The government must call on every school—every parent—every institution and every town to focus our national attention—our resources—our will—on the greatest challenge at the beginning of this century.

The government must help give communities the resources they need to improve their local schools. Most of all, we can, working together, join in a great partnership that challenges every person in America to understand the challenge and to work at the local level to rise up and to meet it.

The government has always helped do for communities what they could not do for themselves. Look at the history of the last century. Look at what we accomplished with leadership from the federal government and commitment from the American people. We passed Social Security—Medicare—a G.I. Bill—the Interstate Highway Act—the Civil Rights Act—the Voting Rights Act—Head Start—national school lunch—100,000 new cops on the street.

At the start of the last century, our public schools had to rise up in the face of new realities and meet the challenges of a changed world.

In 1900, America faced another tumultuous time brought on by the industrial revolution—by hundreds of thousands of immigrants coming to America—by a new world of cities and factories bustling with economic activity. At a time when society was moving from a rural to an urban society, our public schools had to adapt to a new, profoundly different social reality. They did. We did.

In cities, America launched a wave of new school construction, building hundreds of high schools in a few short years. In 1880, we had 800 high schools; ten years later, we had 2,500. Educators developed new classes in subjects like math, science, English, and history, and the innovators—like Calvin M. Woodward in my home town of St. Louis—developed a Manual Training School that helped prepare students for the industrial economy, giving students the tools they needed to succeed in the 20th century.

In 1873, public schools in St. Louis established the first kindergarten classes in the United States. By 1885, St. Louis had 60 kindergarten programs, and by 1910, almost every major city in America had kindergarten in the public schools.

At the dawn of the 21st century, our challenge is to renew that story.

Our challenge is to tap America's bottomless capacity for innovation and hard work to lift up every school in America.

We don't have all the answers. We are not cookie-cutters who believe in a one-size-fits-all approach to local schools. We believe that the federal government can not and should not try to run local schools. Parents are the most important adults in the lives of every child. They care for the children. They inculcate the values. They provide a sense of safety and security to every child, and they must once again be front and center in their child's education.

But government has a responsibility to help—and a capacity to create effective incentives to do what's right for our children. We can facilitate. We can provide leadership and focus. We can dedicate resources for critical priorities. We can foster proven initiatives that successfully encourage maximum flexibility and maximum accountability. We can fight for public schools flexible enough for every parent and accountable to the children who go there.

I'm sure most of you have heard that we are in a tight battle for control of the House of Representatives.

But let me tell you why I feel so passionately about winning a majority.

Six years ago, when we lost the House, Republican leaders put forward radical plans for public education.

They said they would get the government out of our schools, and they followed through on that pledge by trying to abolish the Department of Education.

They reneged on their responsibility to focus on the priorities of the American people.

And a few years prior to that, some Republicans, including their current vice-presidential candidate, went so far as to vote against Head Start and school lunches.

But saying the federal government has no place in our public schools did nothing to lift up a child or help a parent.

The Republican agenda did not succeed because it didn't work, and because the American people rejected it.

The time has come for a new vision.

We must empower families and communities to rally around their children in the ways that are right for them.

We must have as our central purpose and passion making every American child a productive, functional, law-abiding citizen—in a changed world.

We must passionately lead a national bipartisan commitment—almost like World War II—to engage the interest and effort of every institution and every person to ensure—without excuses—that every child will be a productive, functional, law-abiding citizen.

Every family—every institution—every level of government must work together to help schools do all the things they want to do, but can't do.

We will work every day in every way to equip all children to fulfill their human potential.

If we are fortunate enough to win a majority in November, Democrats will make five major new commitments to modernize our public schools and lift up every child.

First, we will help achieve quality education by ensuring that children have qualified teachers and smaller classes. We *must* attract the best and the brightest to be our children's teachers.

My personal experience causes my passion on this issue. My daughter teaches 2 and 3 year old children at Montessori Prep. When she told her friends what she wanted to do with her life, her friends laughed. You want to be a teacher? It doesn't pay. You burn out. There aren't any perks.

Well, my daughter is a terrific teacher—her students love her—and I am so proud of her and her choice.

Democrats will provide financial incentives for 1 million new, fully-qualified teachers and principals over the next decade, and we'll dedicate the resources so that teachers never have to so seriously sacrifice their income just because they want to teach.

We will help schools provide on-going training for teachers, principals, and superintendents.

We will help local schools give teachers incentives to work in inner-cities and other under-privileged communities.

And we will ask the states to establish tests for new teachers to ensure teaching quality, and we will ask them to tie standards to pay to help all teachers become great teachers.

But 1 million new teachers and smaller class size will not get the job done unless our schools are safe.

Democrats will help principals and teachers, school boards and communities make schools safe and drug-free.

We will help by providing additional funding for more after-school, more summer programs, more counselors to prevent violence in schools, more alternative education for children who get suspended or expelled.

And we will ask schools to establish real standards of discipline and behavior, so every teacher and parent can work within their community to get rid of the guns and gangs and return their schools to the mission of education.

But safe schools will not get the job done unless they're also excellent schools with modern buildings and classrooms.

If we win, Democrats will make a major new commitment to help-ing local schools modernize every classroom and every building that needs to be renovated.

We will dedicate new funding for school construction and renova-tion.

We will provide tax incentives that school boards are hungry for so they can modernize buildings and lift up every pupil through better facilities. In exchange for that funding, we will ask the people run-ning the schools to monitor the progress of every child, to make stu-dents accountable for their performance, and to accept responsibility for their school's success.

But modern schools will not lift up every child unless children have the time and attention they need in the early years.

To that end, Democrats will make a major commitment to early childhood education. We want all students to start school ready to read and ready to learn. So we intend to make high-quality early education available to all children.

We will achieve this by making universal pre-school available to all children ages 3 to 5—by improving the pay and skills of child care workers—and by fully funding Early Head Start and Head Start.

Finally, we will help prepare every child for good jobs and successful careers in the Information Age. Our goal is to help prepare America's work-ers for tomorrow's technology, and to help give businesses the human talent they need to succeed and the economy the talent it needs to grow.

We will help bring high tech learning to every classroom and high-skilled workers to every workplace.

We will work with school districts to close the digital divide.

We will help school districts get the expertise and the resources they need to turn around failing schools—to boost the performance of every student— and to close the gap between minorities and non-minorities. We will also dedicate new resources to workforce literacy, technology training partner-ships, employer training networks, and apprenticeship programs, as part of our drive to educate America for the New Economy.

Finally, we will launch an initiative—similar to the post-Sputnik National Defense Education Act—to give children incentives to study science, math, and engineering and to pursue degrees in these fields in college. This pro-gram, like its predecessor, will help inspire a generation of students to go into careers in these important areas, and it will help America remain a glo-bal leader in scientific and medical discoveries.

America is a great country.

We have overcome so many challenges.

But our greatest remaining challenge is to lift up every child and fulfill the human potential of *all* Americans.

Give us this opportunity and it will be done.

The Future Is Now

Education in the Internet Age[3]

Michele Cavataio Sacconaghi

*Vice President of Corporate Relations, AOL Time Warner, Inc., and
Executive Director, AOL Time Warner Foundation; B.A., Brown University; M.P.P., Harvard University; Peace Corps Volunteer in Togo, working on children's health; Chief of Staff to the Deputy Secretary, U.S.
Department of Education; Senior Advisor, Clinton Administration on
race and civil rights issues; at AOL Time Warner, helps the company
use the power of the media, communications, and information technology to serve the public interest.*

Editors' introduction: Michele Cavataio Sacconaghi gave the keynote address at the First Annual Technology in Education Conference
sponsored by ASPIRA. She spoke in the ballroom at the San Juan Hotel
to some 375 educators, directors of educational programs, principals of
schools, and administrators. "What excites me most" about new technology, Vice President Sacconaghi said, "is its potential to increase
access to educational resources for all children." "Technology," she
stated, "is a tool that makes 21st century literacy both possible and
necessary."

Michele Cavataio Sacconaghi's speech: Thank you, Dr. Sala-
gado (Professor, Essex County College), and good afternoon everybody. I am so pleased that ASPIRA has chosen the important topic
of technology and education as its subject for this conference, and I
am honored to be here to share with you my thoughts on this theme.

I am always mindful when I talk about the potential impact of the
Internet, that many of our assumptions about the future of technology don't turn out the way we expect them to.

And that includes predictions from some of the most reliable
sources.

Back in 1939, for example, the *New York Times* claimed that the
problem with an emerging technology called television was that people had to sit in front of it and keep their eyes glued to a screen.
According to the newspaper, the average American family wouldn't
have time for it.

---

3. Delivered in San Juan, Puerto Rico, on December 18, 2000, at lunchtime. Reprinted with permission of Michele Cavataio Sacconaghi.

Of course, not all prophecies are so far off the mark. In 1959, the nation's governors placed a list of predictions inside a time capsule to be opened in 2000. Among their prognoses: In the future, students would have the means to teach themselves.

The truth is, it is fairly easy to forecast what technology will do. After all, most machines are predictable. The hard part is accurately foreseeing what people will do *with* technology. That's the real challenge, and only when we understand the issues affecting how people live, learn and work, will we use technology to truly enhance their lives.

Nowhere is this more evident than in education.

Today, the online medium has the power to transform education from a passive one-on-one process to a unique interactive experience that connects students and teachers all over the world.

Both the rapidly falling prices, and the nonstop expansion, of computing power and bandwidth are making it possible to create and share information in ways we couldn't have anticipated just a short time ago.

Scientists at UCLA, for instance, are developing computer circuits no larger than a few atoms wide. They will enable us to have supercomputers that can fit on the head of a pin . . . or, more practically, in a wristwatch or eyeglasses or traveling through the bloodstream reporting on every activity in the body . . . complete with pictures. Just imagine what you could do in biology class with that.

At the same time, we will be able to move vast amounts of information at incredible speeds. Today, it takes a conventional 28.8 modem a full day to download the contents of the *Encyclopedia Britannica*. Even much faster T-1 lines in large companies require at least several minutes. But the fiber optic strands now being laid down across the country are capable of transmitting the entire Library of Congress in under 30 seconds.

Soon, kids anywhere can have access to one of the world's largest collections of knowledge right at their fingertips.

Indeed, as technology advances, learning in the future will be increasingly based on collaboration and first-hand experiences, without the traditional boundaries set by time or place.

What we all see in this new technology, what excites me most about it—is its potential to increase access to educational resources for all children, and to help all children learn more and learn better.

Technology opens doors to learning that were never possible before. It allows for customized learning environments for children with different learning challenges, whether they are gifted, have special language needs, or have a disability. It can ensure that kids in urban or rural schools that don't have qualified physics teachers can still take an AP Physics course.

It does what traditional textbooks could never do—constantly keep students and teachers up to date on the latest scientific advances without having to continually reprint new editions.

And, most importantly, it is not simply a matter of one-way learning. Technology is at its best when it is interactive.

In the places where all the variables are right, many of us have seen evidence of the benefits of technology first hand. Here is something I've seen, and I bet you have, too: children who are struggling in school, bubble with excitement over the Internet and become more engaged in learning.

But it isn't always easy to get it right.

Our definition of literacy today is rapidly changing. For the first time, in a long time, we are re-evaluating what it means to be literate; what it takes to get there; and how technology plays an essential role.

That is what I would like to talk about this afternoon—what it takes to get the variables right.

When Steve Case started America Online more than a decade ago, few would have predicted the World Wide Web would be the fastest growing technology in economic history. Yet there are now an estimated 350 million people online, and some suggest that number will reach one billion within the next few years.

Fewer still could have imagined how important the interactive medium would be to people's everyday lives. Indeed, our mission is to build a global medium as central to people's lives as the telephone or television; and even more valuable.

But it is the "even more valuable" part of the mission that has driven the company and our work on issues like education. We believe that, while this medium is big enough to matter, it is still young enough to be shaped. And we have an opportunity—in fact, an obligation—to ensure that it enriches people's lives in meaningful ways.

As we work to realize this mission at AOL, we find that we are increasingly dependent on highly skilled and technology-oriented employees.

According to the U.S. Department of Commerce, as many as 60 percent of current jobs require proficiencies in the use of a broad range of information technologies.

Yet demand for skilled technology workers in the U.S. greatly exceeds supply, with more than half of the 1.6 million new technology jobs unfilled. This shortfall means that 1 in every 12 technology jobs has gone vacant this year.

What's more, by 2005, the Bureau of Labor Statistics estimates there will be an additional 70 percent growth in technology-related occupations.

This means the need for technology literacy is critical to our ability to sustain the employee pipeline.

But while virtually every job at AOL requires some familiarity with interactive services, few of our employees are actually specialists in technology.

So we also look to hire employees with strong communication skills and the ability to work in teams. They have to be critical and creative thinkers who can change tasks frequently in a constantly shifting environment. And, most importantly, they must be prepared to be lifelong, adaptive learners.

If our goal were only to ensure a competitive, technology-literate workforce, the task would be formidable enough. But we are equally committed to guaranteeing that today's children are equipped to

---

We must close the digital divide and create digital opportunity in our schools and community-based organizations that serve so many of our kids.

---

meet the challenges of tomorrow's society.

Technology is a tool that makes 21st century literacy both possible and necessary. In bringing technology to schools, there are four objectives we have seen that serve as indicators for success:

The first is attention to equity. New technologies, no matter how powerful, no matter how easy they are to use, will never fully succeed unless they are accessible to everyone, regardless of geography, economics, race, religion or gender.

So we must close the digital divide and create digital opportunity in our schools and community-based organizations that serve so many of our kids. This starts with equitable access to computers and the Internet. Schools and community centers must be equipped with hardware at the classroom level; and it should be connected to the Internet.

Second, we must strive to increase teacher quality and provide opportunities for teachers to enhance their own technology literacy.

The third objective is high quality content. We must focus our schools on delivering such content effectively integrated into learning goals.

And finally, schools need plans that measure progress against specific goals, and administrators who are committed to carrying them out. We still have a lot to learn about how to use technology in the most effective ways. But what we do know is that you have to be focused on the outcomes you want to achieve with technology or you won't ever be able to measure them effectively.

I'd like to talk briefly about these challenges we face in achieving these objectives.

Clearly, there is no other issue as critical to the future of education, and perhaps to the future of the Internet itself, than narrowing the gap between technology haves and have-nots.

It is true, according to the Department of Commerce, that groups that have traditionally been have-nots are making dramatic progress. The gap between rural areas and households nationwide that access the Internet has narrowed from 4% in 1998 to 2.6% in 2000. Moreover, minorities have shown impressive gains in Internet access. Hispanic households, for example, have experienced a significant growth rate: from 12.6% to 23.6%.

Nonetheless, there is still a 17.9 % gap between Hispanics and the national average. And that gap is actually 4% wider now than it was two years ago. Moreover, though one out of every three Americans use the Internet at home, only about one in six Hispanics do so. Plus, the share of Hispanic households with a computer, at 33 percent, is far below the national average of 51 percent.

Today, Americans remain separated by a digital divide based on income, race and ethnicity. Education is an important tool in helping to close this divide. Yet the situation in too many classrooms reflects what is happening in the outside world.

While a record 95% of schools, and 72% of classrooms, are connected to the Internet, many of those classrooms have just one computer, and Internet connections are often somewhere else in the building. That means teachers can prepare classes and give demonstrations, but there is little or no opportunity for students to use the computers themselves.

In 1999, the ratio of students to computers in the poorest schools was 16 to 1, while the nation's wealthiest schools had, on average, 7 students per computer. This is unacceptable. What's more, teachers in high-poverty, high-minority schools are generally more likely than their counterparts elsewhere to encounter problems like outdated or unreliable computers, lack of easy Internet access, and limited IT support.

As leaders who are intricately involved in education, many of you play a major role in using technology effectively, and it is vital that you are provided with opportunities to augment your own knowledge and skills. While leadership and vision are essential to transforming technology into powerful educational tools, we have learned that teachers need support to bring technology successfully into the classroom.

Over the next decade, the retirement rate among teachers will be as high as 75 percent. As a result, we will have to hire and train 2.5 million new teachers just to keep U.S. classrooms properly staffed.

With such a significant rate of turnover, schools of education will have to move aggressively to address the need for pre-service training of new faculty. They must incorporate state-of-the-art educational technology resources to provide high quality training opportunities. And, more importantly, they will have to remake schools of education to meet the needs of the technology-rich classroom.

Yet training opportunities aren't limited just to future teachers. In Washington, D.C., the AOL Foundation is partnering with Trinity College and the District of Columbia Public Schools to build a corps of technology-

Teachers need support to bring technology successfully into the classroom.

trained teachers and administrators. Participants take part in an intensive two-week technology leadership camp where they gain hands-on experience in using technology in the classroom.

At the same time, teachers and administrators take courses at Trinity that prepare them to integrate technology into their lesson plans and to serve as peer mentors in their schools to help other teachers gain expertise.

The pilot program in D.C. is just one of many efforts nationwide to support teachers and provide them with lifelong learning opportunities of their own. But professional development in the use of educational technologies must be deepened and broadened across all sectors of society—especially in underserved communities where teachers are less likely to be credentialed in the fields they teach; and where the risks and implications of falling further behind are so severe.

And while teachers are the linchpins to any successful classroom, they need good material to work with. That is why we launched a grant program called the Interactive Education Initiative.

The IEI provides grants of $7,500 to teams of teachers, administrators, parents and community leaders who have new ideas for using interactive technology to improve student performance. To date, we have awarded about 150 grants to schools and community organizations in 42 states, for projects such as the "Pueblo Gardens Publishing Project" in Tucson, Arizona, which provides opportunities for 330 ethnically-diverse elementary students to publish their fiction, newspapers, artwork and even a multi-cultural cookbook online.

The goal of the Interactive Education Initiative is to seed test beds of innovation at the grassroots level. Ultimately, we hope to identify the most effective models, and enable schools and community organizations to sow the benefits of these efforts in the future.

The IEI is an important first step toward helping teachers to successfully integrate technology into the classroom. And AOL@School is a service that goes many steps further.

AOL@School is a free online educational resource that is organized into 6 portals—one each for primary, elementary, middle school and high school; plus one for teachers and another for administrators. The service takes what AOL does best—aggregating good content and making it easy to use—and makes it readily available for the school audience.

All the content on the site has been rigorously screened by educators. There is built-in, age-appropriate filtering, and teachers can control the extent to which students have access to such tools as email and chat.

When you look at these, and scores of other initiatives by businesses, nonprofits, community and government organizations, you realize the enormous strides we have made in such a short time.

If you think about it, it took 70 years for the telephone to reach 50 million users. That was a lifetime.

It took the computer 20 years, a generation, to reach that same critical mass.

Yet there were 50 million people on the World Wide Web in just 4 years, the time it takes to earn a bachelor's degree.

So we have had a fraction of the time our predecessors had to make this new technology an integral part of our everyday lives. And we have only just scratched the surface.

As we move forward, the future impact of the Internet will remain as difficult to forecast as ever. Indeed, part of the power of the online medium is its randomness, and its ability to take us in altogether unforeseeable directions.

But what will be a lot easier to predict are the consequences if we don't aggressively address the critical challenges we face today.

The digital age presents us with a new set of tools that offer multiple applications and interfaces. It also demands new standards for literacy that forever change how we gather, analyze and communicate information. And it requires us to develop new strategies for how we educate our students and those who teach our students.

At no other time in our history have we had a greater opportunity to fuel our economy, strengthen our democracy and empower our communities. That is why what you are doing at this conference is so important. Bringing together teachers, providers and administrators to discuss how to use this medium will help to ensure that all children have access to a 21st century education. And that is the single most important investment we can make today.

Thank you.

Bringing Hope to Youth

Religious Education for Public School Students[4]

John B. Donovan

Vice President, School Ministries, Inc., and CEO of Donovan-Fitzgerald Speaker Services of New York City; born in Washington, D.C., February 17, 1945, and raised in New York City; M.A., American University, School of International Service, 1975; Marine Corps combat correspondent in Vietnam; journalist with Erie Times, *Pennsylvania; author of* Family Book of Bible Stories, *1986, and* Biography of Pat Robertson, *1988; promotes Released Time religious education nationwide.*

Editors' introduction: Mr. John B. Donovan addressed some 80 directors of religious education from across the United States attending the First National Conference on Released Time Religious Education. The speech was a highlight of the meeting signalling the new surge of interest in Released Time as a means of breaking the cycle of violence among America's youth. Mr. Donovan contends that "religious education" is "the most powerful influence available" for public school students.

John B. Donovan's speech: Good afternoon. You've probably read the newspaper about still another school shooting yesterday. If you're staying at this hotel, you received *USA Today* outside your room, and I want to read the conclusion of just one letter to the editor. A Mr. Willey of New Hampshire writes: "Since we have tried to improve our public school system ineffectively during the past quarter-century by weeding out any moral influence contributed by religion, maybe we should make religious education a more widely accessible option and see how it compares."

Well said, Mr. Willey.

I can tell you right now how it compares. It has been my privilege during the past several weeks to talk with Released Time and after-school religious teachers about the impact they are making on their children. I can say as a citizen that it has been an experience more filled with hope regarding our children than anything I have ever encountered. We can see the Capitol from this window, and we might be reminded how much talk has come from Washington and

---

4. Delivered in Arlington, Virginia, on March 23, 2001. Reprinted with permission of John B. Donovan.

during the presidential campaign about education. It's a sign that people are demanding new solutions to the school problems that confront us, especially those things that pertain to values and virtues, not just to academic subjects. I think the moment has come when it's important to shout from the housetops that it's necessary to reach public school children with the most powerful influence available of a positive nature. That influence is religious education.

If any reasonable person needs evidence of its effectiveness, they simply need to talk to those who have worked in this on a daily basis over a long period of time. The experience of Sr. Evangelista Strohmier in Windber, Penna., would suffice to persuade any intelligent person beyond a reasonable doubt.

She started Released Time classes 18 years ago, and she couldn't believe how ill-mannered her seventh and eighth graders from the public school could be. But she said it was a joy to work with the children in the early grades, and by the time they reached the upper grades, she could compare them with the wild ones she had started with years before. These are still public school children, and not all of them are well-behaved, but the overall contrast is dramatic.

The impact could be characterized as taking place on several levels—individual, interpersonal, and community. When I think of the individual dimension, I think of another quote from today's newspaper—a student saying of the shooter: "He wasn't a popular guy. I heard he was picked on." I also think of the discussions about bullying that became available via the Internet following one of the recent shootings at schools in the San Diego area. Advice came from organizations in New Zealand, the U.K., all over.

Some of the suggestions seemed to have potential practical value, and I won't disparage them. I'll give you an example from a site sponsored by the British Broadcasting Corporation: "Check out your body language. If you stoop, hang you head and hunch over, you may be giving off victim signals. Practice walking with confidence, standing straight with head held high and taking deep breaths."

That advice is fine, as far as it goes. It addresses the issue of confidence, which is very fundamental to us all at every stage of life. But does it go deep enough? Will such advice actually instill the confidence that is often so urgently needed?

Let me suggest an alternative. As part of my work for the National Released Time Bible Education Project, I had occasion to speak with a Catholic Released Time teacher in the rural community of Manchester, Iowa.

Our students can relate very well to the students in the media who said they felt rejected and picked on. They say it happens all the time—not shooting or even fighting but people taking advantage of them." A common pattern for her seventh graders involves older students coming home with them and eating whatever might be available, and then not even looking at them or speaking to them the following day.

Do Released Time classes offer solutions to such widespread and vexing situations? For Wilma, the Scriptures offer a perspective that is available nowhere else: We are created in the image and likeness of God. That's the underlying theme, whether we're teaching about morality, or sacraments, no matter what. There is no reason to feel rejected."

One of the key themes you hear, if you talk with public school teachers or Released Time teachers, is the lack of respect and how basic that is. You don't have to be in education yourself to understand that if there were a high level of respect prevalent in the school systems that the bullying and other forms of antisocial behavior would be minimized.

If you have respect for God and the Scriptures, then you're much more likely to observe certain rules of behavior.

The idea of respect is obviously foundational in religious teaching, because if you have respect for God and the Scriptures, then you're much more likely to observe certain rules of behavior.

Take the case of Patricia Hesdorfer, a Released Time teacher in Levittown, New York, who finds that teaching the commandments is helpful in this regard—as ancient as the Book of Exodus and as up-to-date as the most "with-it" teenager. To Ms. Hesdorfer, the commandment against killing offers important opportunities for her to talk about respect for the body in general, in particular the avoidance of drug abuse. "Also, they understand when I explain that you can kill people in other ways, such as by taking revenge or by saying things that are unkind."

"Children are much more likely to say what they think than they were when I started this in 1965," she says, "and not always in a nice way. But with Released Time programs you get to know them on an everyday basis and all that fades. We just enjoy each other's company."

The commandment against adultery is a chance to talk about the innumerable forms that impurity can take, such as looking at certain magazines and television shows. "We discuss the fact that being popular isn't important, compared with being able to stand up and tell someone that you don't do that kind of thing."

In discussing the commandment to honor your father and mother, she also discusses the need to respect teachers, civil authorities, and their elders in general.

I spoke with another teacher in Houston who majors on the theme of respect also—and she also connects that with the use of drugs and other kinds of inappropriate behavior. Her name is Dora Carrillo.

"We definitely have a lot of drugs in our part of Houston. It's the biggest problem in any poor community. Sometimes even the elementary schools have a police officer," says Dora, a parent and volunteer teacher of religious education programs for Christ the King church. "What we have found is that if you teach them respect, then that keeps them off drugs."

> *"Our battle is to feed our people spiritually."*—Dan Schweiderman, a Released Time teacher

Dora's train of thought goes a level deeper. How does one teach respect, after all? By huffing and puffing with a great show of authority?

Quite the opposite. "Everyone knows who I am here, and I can often relate to children in a way that a teacher cannot by law," she says. "We sit down and read together. We learn prayers together. And we also bring parents into the whole process."

Quite often a spirit of hostility can really be a defensiveness in what people might perceive as an unsafe environment. Consider, for example, the words of a Released Time teacher in a part of New York City dominated by Hispanics, most of them recent immigrants from the Dominican Republic.

"You can see the enthusiasm that kids and parents have about this," Maria says. "They're in a safe place—spiritually and physically." Her church, Incarnation, has become the cultural center for the entire area—the "cathedral of Upper Manhattan" in the words of the late Cardinal John O'Connor. It is now a magnet that draws people from other New York boroughs and even New Jersey.

"One of the keys is that we've done a good job of connecting with our families in their cultural milieu," Dan [Schweiderman] says. Then he cites the tendencies he's up against: "There's still a lot of insensitivity or cultural imperialism. Some institutions are still fighting the battle of the Alamo. But our battle is to feed our people spiritually, and that starts by meeting them at a grassroots level."

Among Hispanics in particular, the building of community is central. The traditional cultural experience is reflected in the "comunidades de base," the environment in which everyone knows and cares about everyone else.

In the view of Dan Schweiderman, a Released Time teacher and organizer, the public schools cannot of themselves leverage the positive values and cohesive power of this without the church, and the church cannot do it very effectively except through programs reaching the public schools. It's a sign of the close relationship between the two institutions in Dan Schweiderman's area that many of the public school teachers are glad to volunteer for religious education programs in after hours.

It is not only the actual instruction that makes the difference but also the positive relational setting in which it is offered. As George Gallup told us here yesterday, the Christian message takes hold best in a relational setting. In Released Time classes and similar after-school programs, the children learn to pray for one another's concerns. Nothing could be more powerful for the building of positive relationships than that.

As expressed by Marge Zipsi, a Released Time teacher in Newhampton, Iowa, learning to relate to each other on a Christian basis is something that the children learn over time. "Then they apply this to their other relationships outside of the Released Time setting."

That in microcosm might sound to many like an answer to our national problem of violence and also to the underlying malaise of which violence is a dramatic symptom.

From this room, we can see the various symbols of our national heritage, including the structures commemorating Lincoln, Washington, and Jefferson. Far in the background, we can also see the great Catholic basilica, the Shrine of the Immaculate Conception, on the right and the Protestant church known as the National Cathedral on the left. Let that symbolize our ecumenical commitment on behalf of this country to go forward today proclaiming the message that religious education is the great answer for our children. Thank you.

Standardized Testing and Its Victims[5]

Alfie Kohn

Author and lecturer; born Miami Beach, FL, October 15, 1957; lives actually in Belmont, MA, and virtually at www.alfiekohn.org; educated at Brown University and the University of Chicago; taught in Massachusetts and Pennsylvania; author of eight books, including: No Contest: The Case against Competition, *1986;* Punished by Rewards, *1993;* What to Look for in a Classroom, *1998;* The Schools Our Children Deserve, *1999; and* The Case against Standardized Testing, *2000; has contributed to most of the leading education periodicals, as well as popular and scholarly publications, such as* Ladies Home Journal, *the* Nation, Harvard Business Review, *and newspapers, including the* New York Times, Washington Post, USA Today, *and the* Boston Globe; *lectures widely to educators, parents, and managers; received American Psychological Association's Award for Excellence in Media, and National Council of Teachers of English's George Orwell Award for Distinguished Contributions to Honesty and Clarity in Public Language.*

Editors' introduction: Having appeared on *Oprah*, *Donahue*, *Today*, National Public Radio, the BBC, and more than 200 other TV and radio programs, Mr. Alfie Kohn was recently described by *Time* magazine as "perhaps the country's most outspoken critic of education's fixation on grades and test scores." He spoke to some 50 scholars, researchers, political activists, and journalists attending a policy forum on standards and testing sponsored by the Cato Institute at its headquarters. Believing that a national dialog was needed concerning educational reforms, Mr. Kohn insisted that "the accountability and standards movement is distinguished primarily by its utter intolerance for disagreement."

Alfie Kohn's speech: Thank you, and thanks for the opportunity to come and address what I believe could accurately be called an educational emergency that we are facing in this country now. Ironically, the emergency has been in large part created in the name of raising standards—not as a result of the kinds of conditions that are used to justify those standards. Let me offer some facts, which I believe are indisputable, and then I will offer some opinions that are disputable.

---

5. Delivered in Washington, D.C., on April 26, 2001, late morning. Copyright © 2001 by Alfie Kohn. Used by permission.

Fact number one is that United States students are tested to an extent that is unprecedented in our history and unparalleled anywhere else in the world. It is perhaps because of that fact that [invited panelist] Kent Talbert's former boss [William Goodling], the Republican former head of the House Education Committee, commented not long ago that if more testing were the answer to the problems in our schools, testing would have solved them a long time ago.

Fact two: standardized tests are primarily measures of the size of the houses near a school. Or, to put it in more technical language, up to 90 percent of the variance in test scores between schools, towns, or states can be explained solely on the basis of socioeconomic status—without even knowing what's going on in the classrooms. To the extent that's true one might respond by saying it is

> *United States students are tested to an extent that is unprecedented in our history and unparalleled anywhere else in the world.*

illegitimate and even unethical to publish (or take seriously) rankings of schools, towns, or states on the basis of test scores.

Third fact. Research has demonstrated repeatedly that there is a positive correlation between how well a kid scores on standardized tests and how shallow his or her thinking tends to be. Researchers have classified kids on the basis of whether they tend to be deep or shallow thinkers—I can talk to you about the criteria if you want—and there has been found to be in elementary, middle, and high school a positive correlation between the shallow approach and how well kids do on standardized tests. It's not a one-to-one correspondence; there are some kids who are deep thinkers and good test-takers, and some kids who are neither, but in general that's the way it works. So higher test scores for an individual student is not usually a good sign.

Fact four. Every major organization in the field of educational measurement has concluded that it is unethical to make high-stakes decisions, such as whether a kid should be flunked and forced to repeat a grade, or denied a diploma at the end of high school, on the basis of a single test or set of tests. The prestigious National Research Council says this, the American Educational Research Association—it is the accepted standard in this field and yet half the states are violating that standard and violating common sense by saying 12 years of academic accomplishment can be irrelevant: you don't pass this test, you don't get a diploma.

Fact five. There is no good evidence that a test-based approach to school reform, let alone high-stakes testing, is effective. The only exception to this is that when you drill kids relentlessly on tests (often to the exclusion of anything else going on in the school) you can raise scores on that test, but it violates basic precepts of educational measurement to use the same test as a lever for accountability and then also as the metric by which to judge whether that approach has been successful. But we do know that states that use high-stakes testing tend to do less well on the National Assessment of Educational Progress than states that do not use high-stakes tests. We have research with individual classrooms that finds when teachers are told they are going to be held accountable for students' test performance, their students tend not to do as well even on the same tests, compared to students taught by teachers with the same curriculum who had instead been given the instruction "See if you can facilitate your students' understanding of this material." We [also] know that dropouts tend to increase when you say to people "You pass this test or else." And there is no evidence suggesting that any kind of testing- or accountability-based approach to education has a positive effect after high school. So, in effect, kids are being used in a kind of giant high-stakes experiment here.

> *Dropouts tend to increase when you say to people "You pass this test or else."*

Last fact, which I think is very hard to dispute, is that the time to raise test scores in schools has to come from somewhere. Where it's coming from now, all over the country, is denying recess to little kids; cutting back on music and the arts; less time for building social and moral skills by having kids participate in class meetings. Or consider current events. Whatever you thought of the last presidential election (followed by a presidential *se*lection), it was a wonderful opportunity for kids to learn about politics, history, math and psychology, and yet I've heard from teachers from all over the place who said, "I would have loved to use this naturally occurring learning opportunity, but there's not going to be any question about today's headlines on the standardized tests, so I couldn't."

Good electives, rich projects that are interdisciplinary—all of these are being scaled back across the country in the name of raising standards, so that when parents hear local officials claim that test scores went up, their first response should be "Oh no, what did you have to sacrifice to make that happen?"

There are degrees of badness in standardized tests.

- You know a test is inadequate if it's mostly multiple-choice, because that doesn't give kids a chance to generate answers or even explain them.

- You know a test is problematic if it's timed, as in, you have 45 minutes to complete this section—because then what you are really measuring is not thoughtfulness, but speed.

- You know a testing system is problematic if standardized tests are given to kids before the end of third grade. I do not know a single reputable expert in the United States in early childhood education who believes that it is legitimate, ethical, or even useful to use standardized tests below that age and I can explain why if you want.

- You know a testing system is problematic if it includes the so-called norm-referenced tests (like the Iowa test, the Stanfords, the Terra Nova, and so on) because those tests were never devised to try to tell you whether kids are learning or whether schools are doing a good job. Those tests were designed to spread out the scores artificially and all you know is who is better than whom—not whether anyone is learning.

- And finally, you know a testing system is problematic if the tests are given every single year, because at that point the tests have cannibalized the curriculum and you have assumed that kids must march in lockstep fashion where every eight-year-old must be here and every nine-year-old must be here, which flies in the face of what we know about child development. It also demands that failures are created. Mandatory annual testing of the kind that the Bush administration has proposed—and, to their shame, that even the opposition has apparently assented to—is an approach that will in effect create failures where they don't have to exist because kids don't all learn and grow at the same pace.

Underlying test-based reform is the notion that harder is the same as better: a kind of mindless, macho approach that says we can judge tests and text and teachers and schools on the basis of whether they're rigorous, challenging, demanding, and tough enough. You hear this kind of language constantly even though a bright six-year-old can tell you that something can be too hard just as surely as it can be too easy. To judge schools primarily on the basis of whether they are sufficiently difficult is like judging an opera on the basis of whether it contains a lot of notes that are really hard for the singers to hit. In other words, it misses most of what matters. And that is indeed the governing mindset these days when high school tests are being offered in some states that I know I couldn't pass, at least not without a lot of pointless cramming. Which raises the question of what Deborah Meier calls Meier's Mandate, namely, that no student should be required to do that which a successful cross-section of adults in the community cannot. To which I would add modestly, Kohn's Corollary to Meier's Mandate, which is that people who talk sanctimoniously about accountability, raising the bar, and tougher standards should be required to take these tests themselves—and have their scores published in the newspaper.

Very quickly I want to offer two myths with respect to standardized testing. Myth one: You need tests for accountability. No knowledgeable educator would ever make such a claim. Never mind the fierce, frantic demands for accountability and where they came from. Let's put that aside. Parents were not sitting around Star-

---

If the notion is we need to make sure that schools are good and they're accountable in the best sense of that term, you don't need a standardized test to do it.

---

bucks one day saying, "You know, our schools need to be held accountable!" Rather, this grew out of a report called "A Nation at Risk" in 1983, which we now know to have been based on misleading and exaggerated evidence, claiming for political reasons that our schools are all failures and setting the stage for the testing fad we find ourselves in now. But if the notion is we need to make sure that schools are good and they're accountable in the best sense of that term, you don't need a standardized test to do it. In fact, you may need the absence of standardized tests in order to create a climate that's about learning instead of fear, that allows students and teachers to demonstrate what's really going on and how much progress is being made—and if you'd like, I'd be happy to talk for hours about more authentic, reasonable, and, indeed, rigorous ways to tell whether students are learning and whether schools are effective. But let us at least make sure that we distinguish sharply between a desire for accountability and the reliance on standardized testing in particular.

The other myth is that you need standardized tests to make sure that poor kids and kids of color are not being neglected. They have been neglected. African-American and Latino kids in the inner cities have been sentenced to second-rate schools to our everlasting shame. But this cure is worse than the disease. It is, in large part, turning these schools into *third*-rate schools, into giant test-prep centers. Visit Houston if you want to see an educational nightmare.

Or, for that matter, Baltimore schools, Chicago schools, where kids are essentially trained seals barking out phonemes on command. Meaningful instruction based on understanding ideas is still going to go on in the rich, white suburbs despite the pressures of testing and accountability. Thus, the gap will grow ever larger.

Then add to this disparity the phenomenon of high-stakes testing where you say to kids, "It doesn't matter if you can demonstrate your competence for years by authentic measures of what you understand: you don't pass this test, you don't get a diploma." The kids will leave. The kids are leaving. In Texas now, partly as a result of high-stakes testing, more than 40 percent of black and Latino ninth graders never get a diploma. In New York City, the dropout rate went up two percentage points last year, and two percentage points the year before that, and is now expected to "skyrocket" according to a report released to the Chancellor's office as a direct result of what is done in the name of closing the gap. Ladies and gentlemen, if we allow high-stakes testing to continue, we are going to face what I would describe as an educational ethnic cleansing in America. And it will all be done in the name of accountability.

The last point I want to address is the notion behind standardized testing that folks in the state capital or in Washington know better. Even if you disagree with almost everything I've said, and you think that standards and tests are terrific, you cannot have a successful policy by having people mandated to do what other people believe is in their best interests. There is plenty of room for disagreement about what constitutes effective educational assessment. I don't pretend to have the answer. But the accountability and standards movement is distinguished primarily by its utter intolerance for disagreement. It is one of the most profoundly undemocratic movements in the history of American education. It reminds me of a sign I saw once on a classroom wall that said, "The beatings will continue until morale improves."

One of the practical effects of this approach is that we are not only pushing kids out of school and not only undermining the most effective curriculum in the name of raising test scores. We are also forcing out teachers. I travel all over this country. I've talked to and listened to educators in almost every state. And let me tell you the teachers who are bailing out are not the mediocre teachers who are afraid of being held accountable. They are some of our most talented educators, who say, "I do not want to be turned into a test-prep technician and have my curriculum dictated by politicians on the local, state, or national level, or by test manufacturers." And they're leaving. To the extent that's true, that is one more respect in which the push for "higher standards" has the effect of lowering standards.

I don't necessarily agree with my hosts here [at the libertarian Cato Institute] that everything can be seen through the lens of "government bad, private sector good." I don't believe the problem here is just government. In fact, I believe that the governmental policies that I've been describing are most pernicious because they follow a private sector model, a series of metaphors and methods that have to do with incentives and sanctions, that have to do with reducing everything to numbers, imposing an assembly-line approach to instruction, and an approach to teaching that is ultimately not about helping kids explore ideas but preparing kids to be workers who will eventually raise the profit of corporations.

We may agree about what government is doing right now. But ultimately, I believe education is a *public* good. We do not make things better by setting people against each other in a vicious and toxic race to defeat each other. Nor do we improve education by treating parents merely as consumers so that learning becomes something like an SUV or a snack that is for sale in the marketplace. But I do believe, and I think we can make common cause here, that what is going on now in terms of national and state top-down, heavy-handed policies is leading a growing number of folks to say this is a disaster for children. We may lose half a generation to this testing fad. These days it seems we can do anything, no matter how silly or counterproductive, as long as we utter the mantras of accountability and rigor and higher standards.

Last week, more than a hundred parents of eighth graders in Scarsdale, New York said, "This is not a matter for writing letters to the editor anymore. This is a matter for civil disobedience." And they refused to have their children participate in New York's testing program. That's going on in inner cities too, from Tucson to Boston, though that didn't make the newspapers. A week from Monday, thousands of students, teachers, and parents from all over New York State—rich and poor, black and white, rural, urban, and suburban—will march on Albany and say, "We want kids to become proficient and engaged learners, but what is going on in the name of standardized testing and accountability not only doesn't help; it actively discourages that." We are indeed facing an educational emergency, which is generating a counterreaction in this country right now, featuring two aspects utterly absent in the accountability movement: democracy and common sense.

Thank you.

A New Direction for Education Reform[6]

Lawrence W. Reed

President, the Mackinac Center for Public Policy, a research and educational organization, Midland, Michigan, 1987– ; born Beaver Falls, Pennsylvania, September 29, 1953; B.A. in economics, Grove City College, 1975, and M.A. in history, Slippery Rock State University, 1978, both in Pennsylvania; taught economics at Midland's Northwood University, 1977–84, chairing the Department of Economics, 1982–84; candidate for U.S. House of Representatives from Michigan's 4th district, 1982; directed Center for the Study of Market Alternatives, Boise, Idaho, 1984–87; has authored hundreds of articles and columns for newspapers, radio, magazines, and journals, as well as five books, including A Lesson From the Past: The Silver Panic of 1893, *1993, and* Private Cures for Public Ills: The Promise of Privatization, *1996; president, State Policy Network of state-based free market think tanks in America, 1994; Board of Trustees, Foundation for Economic Education (FEE), 1994– , and chairman of FEE, 1998–2001; writes a monthly column for FEE's* Ideas on Liberty *entitled "Ideas and Consequences."*

Editors' introduction: The Mackinac Center for Public Policy's (*www.mackinac.org*) mission is to provide a free market perspective on state policies for Michigan citizens and other decision-makers. In a speech to some 200 business and professional people, alumni, and other guests attending a seminar sponsored by Hillsdale College, Lawrence W. Reed, president of the Mackinac Center, applied these principles to education reform.

Lawrence W. Reed's speech: Few issues are more important to the future of this country than the education of our children, and few proposed reforms would do more to improve education than those that would create a truly vibrant, competitive, accountable and hence, choice-driven educational marketplace. More than ever, Americans support the concept of school choice, but exactly what is the best way to achieve it is coming under the microscope. Make no mistake about it—the national school choice movement is at a crossroads, but I will make a case here that a new and exciting direction offers great potential for success.

---

6. Delivered in Boise, Idaho, on May 21, 2001, at a noon luncheon. Reprinted with permission of Lawrence W. Reed. A condensed version of this speech was published in *Imprimis*, the monthly speech digest of Hillsdale College (*www.hillsdale.edu*).

No great cause worth fighting for is accomplished quickly and easily. It may be tempting at times to become discouraged and pessimistic because of a bad turn of events—a negative outcome at the polls in a given election, or a defection from the ranks, for example. To really appreciate larger and longer-term trends, it's important not to let the moment tell the tale. We must mentally turn the clock back not hours, days, or months, but years and even decades sometimes. When we think that way about school choice, it's apparent that we've traveled a great distance.

When Nobel Laureate Milton Friedman first advanced the concept of educational vouchers nearly half a century ago, he was a voice in the wilderness. Few people heard his call and fewer still took him seriously. The overwhelming majority of Americans had become accustomed to government assigning their children to government schools by virtue of their residence, and even when they were unhappy with the results they rarely thought of "choice" as a solution. As the political power of teacher unions grew in the 1960s, it may have seemed then to those in the nascent school choice movement that the odds against them were getting longer, not shorter.

The philosophic and intellectual battle for school choice has been largely won.

But ideas, as Richard Weaver put it, have consequences. Ideas, as Victor Hugo said 100 years earlier, are more powerful than all the armies of the world. They spur revolutions in the political, social, and economic landscape. They change the course of history. They bring down Berlin Walls and whole empires. They take the unmovable and they move it.

A presidential commission awakened the nation in 1983 with this alarming declaration: "If an unfriendly power had attempted to impose on America the mediocre educational performance that exists today, we might well have viewed it as an act of war." A few years later, two scholars—John Chubb and Terry Moe—published a book that put school choice on the frontlines, "Politics, Markets and America's Schools." The choice movement took off, as think tanks, parent groups, and activist organizations devoted to it proliferated.

It is no exaggeration to now say that almost 50 years after Milton Friedman planted the seed, the philosophic and intellectual battle for school choice has been largely won. The ideas of one-size-fits-all or government-knows-best or monopoly-gets-better-results-than-competition are bankrupt. The deplorable outcome of those empty notions is defended by the vested interests whose pockets are lined by the status quo. Parents, taxpayers, and others who are serious about educational quality know better. What is now up for grabs is the practical implementation side of the choice issue. Before exploring that, and offering a promising option, let me summarize the very case for choice itself.

Why Choice Works

The empowerment and transformation of parents into active agents is the foundation of educational choice theory. It's a fact of life that as human beings, we take a greater interest in those things over which we have some power of discretion than in those things we feel relatively helpless to affect. That's why many people spend more time shopping for the car they want—visiting dealership showrooms and comparing prices and features—than they spend in picking the right schools for their children. For a hundred years or more, governments have assigned our children to local public schools based where our homes are; and we pay for those schools whether or not we're able to choose an alternative. That's a strong financial incentive to stay put. The very nature of public, monopolistic bureaucracies is such that raising objections to what the government offers is frustrating, time-consuming and often futile. But when parents are able to say "no, thanks" with speed and ease, they can and will step up to the plate and behave like real consumers of education who are empowered to start shopping around.

Many people spend more time shopping for the car they want . . . than they spend in picking the right schools for their children.

Actually, some parents shop around now. The very wealthy have always had school choice. For them, the price of admission to a good public school may be merely the cost of a moving van and a nice, big house. Or because they can afford to, they will simply pay twice—once in private school tuition and then in taxes for the public system they can reject. A surprising number of poor, inner city families opt for nonpublic alternatives too, but only at enormous sacrifice. Sadly for millions of low-income Americans, education for their children means being stuck with failing and dangerous public schools that spend too much to achieve too little.

A strong correlation has long been noted between parental involvement and the success of children in school. The concept of choice takes full advantage of parents' valuable knowledge about their children and their respective talents, abilities, and learning styles. This information equips parents to make optimal choices about where their children should attend school and what kind of school might best suit their children's needs and temperaments.

Some people say that in an educational system that allows for parental choice, the more thoughtful and involved parents may opt out of a particular school, leaving behind to languish in despair the children of less caring parents. But this ignores the synergy that happens when choice and competition are at work. I like to put it this way: *It takes only a few patrons to leave the restaurant for the chef to get the message to improve the menu.* In other words, choice benefits everybody including those who choose not to fully employ it themselves. That's the magic that has made American free markets the envy of the world.

Why is it that we trust parents in so many areas except education? In our relatively free society, parents decide what foods their children will eat and what foods they will avoid. They decide with whom their children will play, how much television they will watch, and how much homework they will do. The same parents decide which physicians will treat their children's injuries, which dentists will check their teeth, and which babysitters will care for them in their absence. As their children grow, these parents will help them decide which clubs, churches, and organizations to join and which courses of study to pursue. These parents exercise choice when it comes to preschool and higher education, and no one argues that using a government assignment system would make our preschools or colleges better. And yet, many employed by the government school establishment tell us that these very same parents cannot be trusted with choice for grades 1 through 12. That's nothing more than self-serving nonsense.

If Americans had done to the provision of food what they've allowed to happen with their schools, we'd have government farms producing food for sale in government grocery stores. You'd be assigned to one and that's where you would have to buy your groceries. You could patronize a different store, but for the crime of wanting something better for your family, you'd have to submit to the penalty of paying twice. Your assigned government store would get your money whether you shopped there or not. If you wanted to raise objections to what was offered on the shelves, you'd have to wait until the next election, mount an expensive campaign, and cross your fingers. Or, you could line up at boring public meetings and have condescending government officials make you feel antisocial just for showing up. If that had been the way we organized our provision of food a hundred years ago, a presidential commission would have since declared the results akin to an act of war by a hostile foreign power. An ever-expensive, seemingly intractable, national food crisis would fester. And Cambodia would be sending us "Care" packages.

But Americans understood the potent power of choice and competition, left food to the marketplace, and became the best-fed people on the planet. They are now coming to understand, thankfully, that the same principles can apply once again to education.

Three Kinds of Education Reform

Everybody these days is a public school "reformer" because everybody knows that public education needs a fixing at the very least. But not all education reforms are created equal. Indeed, at the Mackinac Center for Public Policy, we believe that all reforms intended to improve the quality of public education fall into just three categories: those dealing with rules, those involving resources, and those concerned with incentives. A comprehensive primer on school choice authored by our director of education policy, Matthew Brouillette, evaluates each approach and also provides point-by-point rebuttals to all the major myths and misconceptions raised by choice opponents.

Rules-based reforms include such things as extending school days and the school year, changing teacher certification and school accreditation requirements, imposing national and state testing, enacting stricter dress codes, and the like. Research has shown that these reforms, while causing marginal improvements, have failed to turn around a large-scale decline in education. More drastic city or state "takeovers" of failing schools and districts and legislative proposals such as "Outcome-Based Education," "Goals 2000," and other regulatory regimes have been and still are being tried, with the same disappointing results.

Another attempted strategy to improve public education is through resource-based reforms. They include such measures as increased funding, new textbooks, wiring schools for Internet access, renovating or updating school facilities, reducing class sizes (fewer pupils per teacher), and other measures that require greater financial expenditures.

Scholars have studied the relationship between per-student spending and achievement test scores since the publication of "Equality of Educational Opportunity" (better known as "The Coleman Report") in 1966. Author James Coleman, a leading sociologist, concluded that factors such as per-pupil spending and class size do not have a significant impact on student achievement scores.

Economist Erik Hanushek and others have replicated Coleman's study and even extended it to international studies of student achievement. The finding of over 30 years of their research is clear: More money does not equal better education. There are schools, states, and countries that spend a great deal of money per pupil with poor results, while others spend much less and get much better results.

Yet, despite this and subsequent findings, many lawmakers and educators continue to believe that additional resources and funding will somehow solve the problems within the government education system.

The Kansas City (Missouri) School District provides the perfect illustration of the inefficacy of increasing resources to improve academic and social outcomes. In 1985, a federal judge directed the district to devise a "money-is-no-object" educational plan to improve the education of black students and encourage desegregation. Local and state taxpayers were ordered to fund this experiment.

The result: Kansas City ended up spending annually more money per pupil, on a cost-of-living adjusted basis, than any of the 280 largest school districts in the United States. The money bought 15 new schools, an Olympic-sized swimming pool with an underwater viewing room, television and animation studios, a 25-acre wildlife sanctuary, a zoo, a robotics lab, field trips to Mexico and Senegal, and higher teacher salaries. The student-to-teacher ratio was the lowest of any major school district in the nation at 13-to-1. By the time the experiment ended in 1997, costs had mounted to nearly $2 billion.

Yet, test scores did not rise. And there was even less student integration than before the spending spree, not more. In May 2000, the Missouri Board of Education officially removed accreditation status from the district for failing to meet any of 11 performance standards. The loss of accreditation means the district has two years to raise test scores, improve graduation rates, and make progress in other areas or face the prospect of a takeover by the state.

We have all but exhausted the "rules" and "resources" approaches to education reform, with little to show for our time and money. The one promising category left is "incentives." Merit pay for teachers is one incentive-style reform. But for reasons I've already pointed out here as well as many more, parental choice is the centerpiece of this strategy. The dramatic growth of charter schools and both intra-district and cross-district public schools-of-choice programs all represent recent introductions of incentive-based reforms. These measures are beginning to replace the rigid assignment system with some important but rather limited choice opportunities.

Giving consumers the opportunity to buy their groceries from the government grocery store of their choice without penalty is certainly better than assigning them to a single public store. But full-blown grocery choice that harnesses the power of a competitive marketplace to maximum advantage is one that removes all political barriers to choice among all options, private grocery stores included. Likewise, full educational choice implies the freedom of parents to pick the best and safest schools—public or private. Parents who place a high priority on education for their children would be empowered or incentivized, not penalized.

Vouchers

Milton Friedman was the first major American figure to sketch a vision of full educational choice, and the vehicle he proposed for achieving that vision more than 40 years ago (and one he still champions to this day) is the *voucher*. Public, tax-funded vouchers are simply direct payments from the government to individuals to enable them to purchase a particular good or service—in this case, education—in the open market. Those payments can be in the form

---

Full educational choice implies the freedom of parents to pick the best and safest schools—public or private.

---

of a check that the beneficiary deposits in his bank account and draws upon to pay for the vouchered item. Or, they can be a coupon that the beneficiary gives to the private provider of the vouchered item, who then redeems it for cash from the government.

Food stamps are a well-known example of vouchers. When Congress started the program in the 1960s, it could have gone in another direction. To help low-income people get food, it could have set up those government grocery stores I've already mentioned, and then required the poor to get their food there. But in the interests of keeping costs down, keeping quality high, and allowing recipients the benefit of choice, the Congress created food stamps instead. I'm very well aware of all the valid moral and economic arguments against food stamps and the subsidy they represent, but let's face it: they beat Soviet supermarkets hands down.

We should note that vouchers aren't always creatures of government. Pioneered by such philanthropists as Peter Flanigan and J. Patrick Rooney, privately funded vouchers (sometimes called scholarship programs) are now making it possible for tens of thousands of children to opt out of bad public schools and into good private ones. Such programs have the inherent virtue of being entirely voluntary every step of the way. Bureaucracy for its own sake doesn't exist within such programs. And because no tax money enters the picture, there are no politicians piling on the paperwork, meddling with the schools, or otherwise using the education of the children involved as a political football. But the real debate over vouchers for school choice centers on publicly funded ones.

Public voucher programs are in place in Milwaukee, Cleveland, certain rural communities within the state of Vermont, and in a very limited way in Florida. Parental satisfaction is high and studies are beginning to show that the programs are yielding improvements in student performance. But at the same time, the future of the voucher option is cloudy and uncertain. Legal and constitutional challenges are numerous. The opposition has succeeded in stigmatizing vouchers to the point where "the V-word" is shunned even by proponents. President Bush could not get the Congress to fund even

---

> ### *The opposition has succeeded in stigmatizing vouchers to the point where "the V-word" is shunned even by proponents.*

---

a tiny voucher program. A significant number of private schools that would be eligible for vouchers don't want to touch them with the proverbial 10-foot pole, in fear of the attached strings.

And it's becoming abundantly evident that while vouchers may be politically feasible in a few legislatures, they are dead-on-arrival when attempted at the ballot box. No voucher initiative—and there have been many of them—has ever secured much more than 30 percent of any popular vote, even as polls show strong majority support for the general concept of choice at the same time.

Increasingly within the school reform movement, vouchers are no longer seen as the one and only way, or even the best way, to realize full educational choice. There is, in my view, a superior option that is not only better policy but is more politically viable as well. That option is tax credits.

Tax Credits

Tax credits are designed to provide parents with tax relief linked to expenses incurred when they select a school other than the government-assigned one for their children. That typically means a private school, but tax credits can also apply to tuition charged by a public school that accepts a student from outside its regular jurisdiction. The credit is usually a dollar-for-dollar reduction in taxes owed (whereas a tax *deduction* is merely a reduction in taxable income). For example, if a taxpayer has a pre-credit tax liability of $2,000 and a tuition tax credit of $1,500, the taxpayer would pay a tax of only $500.

Tax credits are typically applied against only state and/or federal income taxes, but property tax credits have been proposed as well. For the purposes of school choice, tax credits might be allowed for any or all out-of-pocket educational expenses incurred by an individual, from tuition to textbooks to transportation to extracurricular fees—though tuition is the most common expense allowed in practice. Private schools usually charge tuition and/or fees, and government schools often charge tuition to nonresident students and fees for extracurricular activities. These expenditures are also creditable items under many tax credit proposals.

Many proponents of educational tax credits prefer them to vouchers on the grounds that they entail less government regulation of private schools and less risk of entanglement between church and state because of their indirect nature. Credits, unlike vouchers, do not transfer any money from the state to schools or taxpayers. There's no need to launder anybody's money through a public bureaucracy first before it pays for a child's schooling.

Indeed, because vouchers are funded out of the pool of taxpayer funds, some citizens will always argue that "Some of *my* money will be going to send *your* child to a school I don't like." Those citizens will want government to regulate how, when, and where their tax money can be used by other people. The legislators who appropriate it and the bureaucracy that dispenses it will be more than happy to oblige.

Because of the prospect of regulation, some private schools will surely not accept vouchers—at first. But over time, it will become very difficult for them to pass up the allure of "free" money and the opportunity to make schooling less expensive for their families. Government shackles will follow government shekels, as they always do sooner or later. With private schools increasingly dependent on voucher revenue, few will be able to wean themselves away when regulation becomes invasive. The initial benefit of competition between schools due to vouchers will diminish as regulation homogenizes all schools into an amorphous blob feeding at the public trough.

Tax credits, on the other hand, don't represent a claim by anyone on someone else's wallet. You don't get the credit if you don't pay tuition or if you don't pay taxes. A credit on your taxes represents your own money, period.

Education researcher and author Andrew Coulson notes that a significant advantage tax credits have over vouchers is that they restore to the family the direct financial responsibility for educating their children. He writes, "Since all the money involved in these [tax credit] programs is privately and voluntarily spent, issues of church-state entanglement and necessary public oversight of public spending are rendered moot. Because of the greater resistance to regulation that follows from the absence of state funding under tax-credit programs, those programs do a better job. . . ." Coulson argues that tax credits are superior to vouchers because they more effectively promote and protect the conditions that have historically produced educational excellence: parental choice, direct parental financial responsibility, freedom for educators, competition among schools, financial incentive for educators, and universal access to the education marketplace.

Tax credits are mechanisms for fairness.

Here's another way to see this crucial difference: Vouchers are food stamps for education, a mechanism for the forcible redistribution of wealth from all citizens to some citizens. Tax credits are mechanisms for fairness, an accounting device that permits people to keep at least some of their own money that they would otherwise pay for the government-assigned school they are not using. Moreover, if the credit allowed is a modest one—half, for example, of what the government spends per pupil in the public system—then an actual savings for the public system and for all taxpayers is generated every time a child migrates from a public school to a private one. All of that makes it impossible for opponents to argue honestly that the tax credit is "draining" funds from the public system, though the more dishonest among them will say that anyway.

In the long run, vouchers may not diminish the role of government and politics in education. Tax credits are much more likely to reduce that role and to put private institutions and private individuals—parents in particular—in charge once again. But while both mechanisms are worth the risk to escape the intolerable *status quo*, both still require vigilance to keep the government at bay.

Political Viability

Friedman has said he prefers vouchers over tax credits because we should not use the tax system as a social engineering tool. But a tax credit for education is fundamentally different from a tax credit for solar panels or electric cars or any other politically correct gimmick du jour. That's because not only is education itself mandatory, but taxes to pay for it are as well, and that's not likely to change any time soon. A tax credit designed to get you to change your behavior (to buy a solar panel, for instance) is just not the same as a tax credit that refunds some of what government charged you for something you don't want to buy.

Instinctively, most people seem to understand this distinction. They are naturally more sympathetic to the fairness of a tax credit than the redistribution of a voucher. They are much more familiar with tax credits and their kissing cousin—tax deductions—because they've used them again and again year after year. When a survey of congressional and state legislative candidates was done in my state in 1998, we found many incumbents and challengers who favored tax credits for education but not vouchers, and none who favored vouchers but not tax credits.

When a voucher plan was on the ballot in Michigan in November 2000, yard signs popped up all over the state declaring "No Vouchers!" It's hard to imagine a similar proliferation of "No Tax Credits!" signs, had that been the choice before voters. Even liberal Democrats like Bill Clinton, Al Gore, and our new U.S. Sen. Debbie Stabenow support tax credits for preschool and post-grade 12 education.

Not surprisingly, of all the many statewide ballot initiatives for educational choice across the nation in the past 30 years, the one that holds the record for securing the greatest percentage of the popular vote is the 1998 Colorado tax credit initiative (about 41 percent). It was poorly crafted, vastly underfunded, and it came out way too late for its proponents to have enough time to inform the public. But it still beat by a good margin the highest vote percentage any voucher plan has ever won.

Yes, any tax credit adds a complication (a line or two) to our tax forms, and thereby takes us a step away from a less complicated flat tax. As a staunch advocate of limited government, free markets, and a flatter income tax if we're going to have one at all, I confess to a small strategic compromise there. But our voucher friends need to acknowledge that vouchers are a whale of a bigger fudge than any tax credit. Most voucher proponents don't advocate food stamps, redistribution, or government subsidies for any other business or enterprise. A tax credit for education is not so much a compromise as it is simply the best mechanism we're likely to get for letting people keep what's theirs when they are paying taxes for education but don't want to buy it from the government.

Tax credits for education can assume different shapes. Under a traditional credit plan, only a parent who pays private educational expenses (like tuition) for his child and who has a tax liability greater than the amount of the allowable credit will qualify. The problem with a traditional tax credit is that low-income parents who don't have the money to pay for a private school or have little or no tax liability will be left out in the cold. That deficiency could be remedied partially by making the credit "refundable," meaning the credit could result in a refund check from the government if your tax liability is low. But that would effectively voucherize the tax credit insofar as low-income parents are concerned, which would introduce some of the political and economic baggage of vouchers that I've already mentioned.

The form of tax credit that solves these problems is one for which my organization, the Mackinac Center for Public Policy, is nationally known for pioneering as early as 1996. We were the first to give it the name, "Universal Tuition Tax Credit," and the first to design such a plan for an entire state—Michigan. It will require an amendment to our state constitution, which I forecast will happen in the future, but until that day comes I'm happy to report that the concept is catching on elsewhere.

In states like Virginia, Utah, and Idaho, groups have copied or adapted the Mackinac plan to their particular state's tax and education funding infrastructures, and are gaining public and legislative attention for these adaptations. Our senior vice president and chief architect of the plan, Joseph Overton, predicts this approach will eventually eclipse all others as the preferred vehicle for achieving full educational choice. The Cato Institute in Washington has endorsed the basic framework of the Mackinac plan and is working with us to get it a wider hearing nationally.

Key to our "universal" tax credit concept is that it allows any taxpayer—individual or corporate, parent or grandparent, neighbor or friend—to contribute to the education of any elementary or secondary child and then qualify for a dollar-for-dollar credit against certain taxes owed. The maximum credit is equal to half what the government spends per pupil in the public schools, which is more than enough to cover educational expenses at 90 percent or more of private schools. It envisions scholarship funds supplied with private tax credit monies. These scholarship funds would be established by schools, companies, churches, and myriad private groups—spurred on by individuals and companies who want to help children get their schooling in the best and safest schools of their choice.

Would tax credits be sufficient to encourage businesses to contribute to education scholarship funds? Absolutely. After explaining the concept, I've asked CEOs all over our state this question: "Suppose you had a choice. You could send a million dollars in taxes to Lansing for the politicians to spend. Or, you could send that million to one or more scholarship funds to help children who might be your future employees get a good education. Which would you do?" I've never met one who preferred option #1.

The popularity of tax credits among parents has exploded throughout the country in recent years. K–12 tax credits have passed state legislatures in Arizona, Minnesota, Iowa, and Illinois. Arizona expanded parental school choice in 1998 to include tax credits for donations to both private scholarship programs and government schools. Former Gov. Fife Symington signed into law a bill in April 1997 granting an income tax credit of up to $500 for people who donate to nonprofit groups that distribute private scholarships to students. The law also offers taxpayers a credit of up to $200 for money given to government schools to support extracurricular activities.

Michigan Congressman Peter Hoekstra is proposing federal legislation that would permit a universal education tax credit of up to $500 against federal income taxes owed. That would keep billions of dollars from ever going to Washington in the first place, which is a virtue in itself. But education is still overwhelmingly a state and local matter, and that's where groups must work to craft a universal tax credit plan onto their existing tax and education infrastructure. That is now starting to happen, and in the wake of the crushing defeat last year of two well-funded, big-state voucher referenda (California and Michigan), I predict it will soon snowball.

One final thought: Any school choice plan should start with the recognition that private schools are not the problem we face today. They are an important part of the solution. We must not bargain away their independence to get choice even if it's in the form of a universal tax credit. We must not burden them with new government mandates cloaked in the guise of "accountability." Private schools are already accountable—they have customers who can take a walk, not captives who have no real options.

Educational choice is an idea whose time has come, and the universal education tax credit is an idea whose time is about to arrive. It can get the job done and avoid many of the problems inherent in the voucher approach. It will minimize the danger of intrusive government, though private schools will always have to be vigilant under any system. It will galvanize and strengthen civil society by giving individuals and companies new incentive to assist the educational dreams of their fellow citizens. It will bolster the incentives of existing public schools to improve. And perhaps most importantly, it will put choice and responsibility back in the laps of parents from whom such things should never have been taken in the first place.

Get involved. Make the case. Talk to your friends, your neighbors, and your legislators. Join the growing army of concerned parents who want real educational choice. If we win this, we'll no longer have an education system that looks like a hostile foreign power imposed it on us. We'll have a world-class system that leaves no child behind.

IV. Diversity

Thoughts on Building a House for Diversity[1]

Antoinette M. Bailey

Vice President, Community and Education Relations of The Boeing Company; undergraduate degree, Southern Illinois University–Carbondale; masters degree, Michigan State University; former president, Boeing-McDonnell Foundation; prior to merger served as Human Resource Division Director for McDonnell Douglas Aerospace East; Chairperson, Contributions Committee of the Conference Board; board member Urban League of Metropolitan St. Louis, and YWCA of Metropolitan St. Louis.

Editors' introduction: Antoinette M. Bailey addressed the Third Annual Cultural Diversity Conference at Lincoln University sponsored by the Missouri Department of Natural Resources. Vice President Bailey asked for the "same kind of dedication to diversity in the purely human and organizational context" that many bring "to diversity in the . . . environmental context."

Antoinette M. Bailey's speech: I'd like to begin by retelling a story that was told in the late 70s and early 80s, when there was great pessimism about the ability of U.S. companies to compete in the global marketplace. Bear in mind: This was before E-Bay, Priceline, Amazon, and all the other dot.com companies. It was before the World Wide Web. It was before the invention of the microprocessor. Americans were under siege—or so we felt at the time—from everything from high-priced oil to low-priced automobiles and appliances from abroad.

So here is the story. Three businessmen—a Frenchman, a Japanese man, and an American—are lined up before a firing squad. According to ancient custom, each is granted a final wish. The Frenchman says he would die happy if he could sing "La Marseillaise" one more time. He does . . . and he sings this old revolutionary song so well that it brings tears to the eyes of the riflemen. Even so, they take steady aim and shoot the Frenchman dead.

The Japanese businessman is inspired by the patriotic example of the Frenchman. He expresses his desire to give one last speech on "Kaizen," the Japanese word for encouraging incremental improvements in the production system. However, before he can get started,

---

1. Delivered in Jefferson City, Missouri, on March 17, 2000, in the morning. Reprinted with permission of Antoinette M. Bailey.

the American rises and insists that he be the next to go. "I will die happy," says the American, "if I don't have to listen to one more lecture on Japanese Management."

When Kenneth Seeney invited me to speak at this gathering, I must admit that my first inclination was to say no. I was not sure that I wanted to be the instrument of subjecting all of you to one more lecture on the importance of diversity. Diversity, with a capital "D," has become one of the buzzwords in American businesses and society . . . and anything that "buzzes" is likely to be a source of annoyance, whether it is a swarm of mosquitoes, or the insistent and indiscriminate use of certain words and phrases.

Beyond that, I was not sure that I would be the right person to connect with you as an audience. To be perfectly frank, you are looking at the consummate urban dweller. I enjoy the beauty of nature and I appreciate the fragility of our environment, but I have never pitched a tent, climbed a mountain, run a fast river, or done many of the other things that many of you probably take for granted.

However, as I was pondering all this, it dawned on me that we do share a passionate sense of conviction about one thing.

With this audience, I don't have to point out the importance of another kind of diversity, which is to say, bio-diversity. You know the terrible dangers posed by pollution and wasteful management of natural assets in the destruction of habitats and the extinction of many forms of life. You are the real experts when it comes to appreciating the beauty that exists in the larger mosaic of life. We are a species that relies on insects to pollinate many of our crops and we can thank the accumulated masses of bacteria that lived over billions of years ago for our primary sources of energy (oil and gas). We owe the very air we breathe to the photosynthetic activities of those same bacteria.

As a native Missourian, I know that this is an extraordinary state in terms of ecological and biological diversity. It has everything from swamp lands and river delta on the east to tall grass and plains on the west. It has a northern portion above the Missouri River that marks the farthest advance of the glaciers, and a southern portion that includes an ancient volcanic mountain range and an uplifted eroded plateau that is famously known as "the Ozarks." You in the Missouri Department of Natural Resources, along with your colleagues in the Department of Conservation, are the true stewards . . . and champions . . . of this amazing diversity.

So my message to you this morning is really very simple. It is to bring the same kind of thinking . . . and the same kind of dedication . . . to diversity, in the purely human and organizational context, that you already do to diversity, in the biological and environmental context.

The same thinking applies in both spheres. We value diversity in the biological realm because we know that there is strength in diversity. Greater diversity means a superior gene pool through greater variation and complexity. It means both more competition and more cooperation between species. It means greater adaptability . . . along with stiffened natural resistance to disease and great disasters of one kind or another.

We at Boeing value diversity for the exact same reasons. We are a company with a population of nearly 200,000 people, with operations in 27 states (most assuredly including Missouri), and with customers in no fewer than 145 countries. But we do not assume that diversity is something that comes with the territory in being big and being active around the globe. To the contrary, we are spending a

---

The true test of diversity within an organization . . . is whether people build upon their differences . . . or whether they are divided or even destroyed by them.

---

great deal of time, money, and effort to become more diverse at all levels of our organization. This is not simply—or cynically—a matter of compliance. We want people to think and act differently . . . to act with greater speed, agility, and creativity. Those attributes are required in an increasingly complex and demanding global business environment. In a self-interested way, we, too, have come to the conclusion that there is strength in diversity.

How do you encourage diversity? Above all, how do you encourage it in an organizational setting, such as Boeing or the DNR? Large organizations are different from the habitats found in nature in the sense that they are (and I'm not intending to be gender-specific when I say this) man-made constructs. They are what we make them.

Diversity is about us . . . each and every one of us. The point is not that there are differences. The point is whether we can learn from those differences. The point is not that there are varying viewpoints, but whether we can recognize and respond to those varying viewpoints.

Perhaps we should examine the key word a little more closely. According to the dictionary, "diversity" simply means difference, unlikeness, or variety. Like the proverbial snowflake, each of us is different—in some way, unique. However, again like the snowflake, we are also incredibly alike. For all of the differences between people, far less than 1% of our DNA separates any one human being from any other.

The true test of diversity within an organization . . . or across a whole society . . . is whether people build upon their differences . . . or whether they are divided or even destroyed by them. Part of the greatness of our country is contained in the motto that is stamped on our coinage—E Pluribus Unum, Out of Many One. Conversely, in a place like Yugoslavia, the tragedy has been the failure of a people who are racially and in other ways the same to bridge their differences in religion and history.

Skin color, gender, age, and sexual orientation are some of the obvious and important differences between people. But there are many other differences in background, history, and habit that are also profoundly important . . . and that must be addressed in any organization that wants to reap the benefits of diversity.

About ten years ago, I was a co-leader of a study examining why it was that so many promising young African-Americans seemed to veer off course . . . in terms of their career development . . . within a few years of being hired. These were people who had earned top grades at top universities . . . and who appeared to be every bit as qualified as their white counterparts at the outset of their employment. What we found was that promising African-Americans, unlike promising whites, had been largely ignored by their white supervisors. This happened not out of a spirit of viciousness, but more out of avoidance. The white front-line managers simply didn't feel comfortable dealing with young black people. So they seldom tried to challenge or engage them.

This brings me to a favorite book . . . and I recommend it to all of you. It's called *Building a House for Diversity*. The author is R. Roosevelt Thomas, Jr., and we have retained him as a consultant in building a house for diversity at Boeing.

Thomas's book begins with a wonderful fable about a giraffe who wants to befriend an elephant and who therefore invites the elephant into his house. After some quick carpentry to enlarge the basement door in order to admit the elephant, the giraffe goes off to answer a phone call, telling the elephant, "Please make yourself at home." But every time the elephant moves, there is a large scrunch or crashing sound. When the giraffe returns, he is amazed at the damage that the elephant has done and is quick to offer advice. Sign up for weight-watchers, he urges the elephant. And it wouldn't hurt, he adds helpfully, "if you'd go to ballet class at night" . . . in order to become "lighter on your feet."

There are three clear morals to be drawn from the interaction between the giraffe, as the insider, and the elephant, as the outsider. The first is the silliness of expecting an elephant to assume the same dimensions as a giraffe. If you are serious about diversity, you should build your house with that in mind. But that is not the easiest of tasks. As a second moral to the story, you should expect a certain amount of tension and complexity. And finally, each of us must be prepared to move outside our original comfort zone if we want to embrace

> *Diversity is . . . the powerful presence of a sense of teamwork and community.*

and promote diversity. That's the third and biggest moral from the story. There is no such thing as a diverse organization created by executive dictate. It is something that will come into being only through the willing and active behavior of supervisors, managers, and people at all levels.

But I suspect that most of you have already learned those same lessons in managing the great physical resources of this state. It wouldn't occur to you to think that every stream was the same or that every forest was the same. You accept the need for positive actions dictated by unusual soil conditions or other localized differences. Say there has been substantial erosion of topsoil in a place of rich farmland. That could be an action that would elicit some kind of counter-action on your part. And I trust that we can all agree that the maintenance of a clean environment requires the concerted efforts of all concerned citizens.

When I—as an African-American, female, corporate executive—speak on the topic of diversity, I know that there is always going to be an unspoken question on the minds of many listeners. They will wonder: What does she really think? If I could take away her script and read her inner thoughts, what would they be?

I will try to answer that question with particular reference to race.

Frankly, I am worried. What makes me apprehensive is the growing gap in the perceptions of white Americans on one side and black Americans on the other. It is as though the giraffe and the elephant have each been blinded to what the other sees as reality. White Americans, for the most part, believe that race is no longer much of an issue in our society. They see the nighttime television dramas in which individuals from all races get along as buddies and excel equally. That's how it is in real life, right?

Wrong, I would tell you. While I cannot pretend to speak for black Americans as a whole, I can tell you that a recent Gallup poll indicates that 50% of black Americans believe that they have been discriminated against within the past 30 days . . . when shopping, dining out, working, using public transportation, or interacting with the police. What's more, I can cite studies showing that, with similar educational backgrounds, black males earn less than 75 percent of what their white peers take home.

Our journey toward greater harmony and justice is not yet over.

Having already given you the dictionary version, I would like to close with my own definition of diversity. To my mind, diversity is not merely the absence of discrimination; more fundamentally, it is the powerful presence of a sense of teamwork and community . . . one that brings all kinds of people from different backgrounds together . . . with the end result of creating a whole that is much greater than the sum of the individual parts.

My challenge to you—who are already fighting on the side of the angels when it comes to the environment—is be equally bold and energetic in bringing that kind of teamwork and community into play . . . in making the Missouri Department of Natural Resources a true house for diversity.

To Reunite a Nation[2]

Patrick J. Buchanan

Journalist, radio and television commentator, and author; honors graduate in English and philosophy, Georgetown University, 1961; Masters in Journalism, Columbia University, 1962; Special Assistant to President Richard Nixon, 1969–74; Special Assistant to President Gerald Ford, 1974; Communications Director for President Richard Nixon, 1985–87; author of Right from the Beginning, *1988; syndicated columnist (150 newspapers); moderator, CNN's* Capital Gang; *co-host, CNN's* Crossfire; *panelist,* The McLaughlin Group; *host, Mutual Radio's* Buchanan & Co. *(160 stations).*

Editors' introduction: While campaigning for president of the United States in 2000, Mr. Patrick J. Buchanan ran on an agenda of "putting America, and Americans, First!" If elected, he promised to "end foreign aid," "halt cold the invasion of illegal aliens into the U.S.," "maintain peace through strength," "eliminate affirmative action and quotas," "appoint conservatives to the Supreme Court," and "restore prayer and the Bible to our schools." Mr. Buchanan's speech, part of the Nixon Library's Distinguished Speaker's Series, was attended by about four hundred people gathered in the Nixon Library. Mr. Buchanan cautioned that "a country that cannot control its borders isn't fully sovereign."

Patrick J. Buchanan's speech: Let me begin with a story: In 1979, Deng Xiaoping arrived here on an official visit. China was emerging from the Cultural Revolution, and poised to embark on the capitalist road. When President Carter sat down with Mr. Deng, he told him he was concerned over the right of the Chinese people to emigrate. The Jackson-Vanik amendment, Mr. Carter said, prohibited granting most favored nation trade status to regimes that did not allow their people to emigrate.

"Well, Mr. President," Deng cheerfully replied, "Just how many Chinese do you want? Ten million. Twenty million. Thirty million?" Deng's answer stopped Carter cold. In a few words, the Chinese leader had driven home a point Mr. Carter seemed not to have grasped: Hundreds of millions of people would emigrate to America in an eyelash, far more than we could take in, far more than our existing population of 270 million, if we threw open our borders.

---

2. Delivered in Yorba Linda, California, on January 18, 2000, at 10:30 a.m. Reprinted with permission of Patrick J. Buchanan.

And though the U.S. takes in more people than any other nation, it still restricts immigration to about one million a year, with three or four hundred thousand managing to enter every year illegally.

There is more to be gleaned from this encounter. Mr. Carter's response was a patriotic, or, if you will, a nationalistic response. Many might even label it xenophobic. The President did not ask whether

> *America is Balkanizing as never before.*

bringing in 10 million Chinese would be good for them. He had suddenly grasped that the real issue was how many would be good for America? Mr. Carter could have asked another question: Which Chinese immigrants would be best for America? It would make a world of difference whether China sent over 10 million college graduates or 10 million illiterate peasants, would it not?

Since the Carter-Deng meeting, America has taken in 20 million immigrants, many from China and Asia, many more from Mexico, Central America and the Caribbean, and a few from Europe. Social scientists now know a great deal about the impact of this immigration.

Like all of you, I am awed by the achievements of many recent immigrants. Their contributions to Silicon Valley are extraordinary. The over-representation of Asian-born kids in advanced high school math and science classes is awesome, and, to the extent that it is achieved by a superior work ethic, these kids are setting an example for all of us. The contributions that immigrants make in small businesses and hard work in tough jobs that don't pay well merits our admiration and deepest respect. And, many new immigrants show a visible love of this country and an appreciation of freedom that makes you proud to be an American.

Northern Virginia, where I live, has experienced a huge and sudden surge in immigration. It has become a better place, in some ways, but nearly unrecognizable in others, and no doubt worse in some realms, a complicated picture over all. But it is clear to anyone living in a state like California or Virginia that the great immigration wave, set in motion by the Immigration Act of 1965, has put an indelible mark upon America.

We are no longer a biracial society; we are now a multi-racial society. We no longer struggle simply to end the divisions and close the gaps between black and white Americans; we now grapple, often awkwardly, with an unprecedented ethnic diversity. We also see the troubling signs of a national turning away from the idea that we are one people, and the emergence of a radically different idea, that we are separate ethnic nations within a nation.

Al Gore caught the change in a revealing malapropism. Mr. Gore translated the national slogan, "E Pluribus Unum," which means "Out of many, one," into "Out of one, many." Behind it, an inadvertent truth: America is Balkanizing as never before.

Five years ago, a bipartisan presidential commission, chaired by Barbara Jordan, presented its plans for immigration reform. The commission called for tighter border controls, tougher penalties on businesses that hire illegal aliens, a new system for selecting legal immigrants, and a lowering of the annual number to half a million. President Clinton endorsed the recommendations. But after ethnic groups and corporate lobbies for foreign labor turned up the heat, he backed away.

The data that support the Jordan recommendations are more refined today. We have a National Academy of Sciences report on the economic consequences of immigration, a Rand study, and work by Harvard's George Borjas and other scholars. All agree that new immigration to the United States is heavily skewed to admitting the less skilled. Unlike other industrialized democracies, the U.S. allots the vast majority of its visas on the basis of whether new immigrants are related to recent immigrants, rather than whether they have the skills or education America needs. This is why it is so difficult for Western and Eastern Europeans to come here, while almost entire villages from El Salvador have come in.

Major consequences flow from having an immigration stream that ignores education or skills. Immigrants are now more likely than native-born Americans to lack a high school education. More than a quarter of our immigrant population receives some kind of welfare, compared to 15 percent of native-born. Before the 1965 bill, immigrants were less likely to receive welfare. In states with many immigrants, the fiscal impact is dramatic. The National Academy of Sciences contends that immigration has raised the annual taxes of each native household in California by $1,200 a year. But the real burden is felt by native-born workers, for whom mass immigration means stagnant or falling wages, especially for America's least skilled.

There are countervailing advantages. Businesses can hire new immigrants at lower pay; and consumers gain because reduced labor costs produce cheaper goods and services. But, generally speaking, the gains from high immigration go to those who use the services provided by new immigrants.

If you are likely to employ a gardener or housekeeper, you may be financially better off. If you work as a gardener or housekeeper, or at a factory job in which unskilled immigrants are rapidly joining the labor force, you lose. The last twenty years of immigration have thus brought about a redistribution of wealth in America, from less-skilled workers and toward employers. Mr. Borjas estimates that one half of the relative fall in the wages of high school graduates since the 1980s can be traced directly to mass immigration.

At some point, this kind of wealth redistribution, from the less well off to the affluent, becomes malignant. In the 1950s and '60s, Americans with low reading and math scores could aspire to and achieve the American Dream of a middle class lifestyle. That is less realistic today. Americans today who do poorly in high school are increasingly condemned to a low-wage existence; and mass immigration is a major reason why.

There is another drawback to mass immigration: a delay in the assimilation of immigrants that can deepen our racial and ethnic divisions. As in Al Gore's "Out of One, Many."

Concerns of this sort are even older than the Republic itself. In 1751, Ben Franklin asked: "Why should Pennsylvania, founded by the English, become a Colony of Aliens, who will shortly be so numerous as to Germanize us instead of our Anglifying them?" Franklin would never find out if his fears were justified. German immigration was halted by the Seven Years War; then slowed by the Great Lull in immigration that followed the American Revolution. A century and half later, during what is called the Great Wave, the same worries were in the air.

> *It is impossible not to notice the conflicts generated by a new "hyphenated Americanism."*

In 1915 Theodore Roosevelt told the Knights of Columbus: "There is no room in this country for hyphenated Americanism. . . . The one absolutely certain way of bringing this nation to ruin, of preventing all possibility of its continuing to be a nation at all, would be to permit it to become a tangle of squabbling nationalities." Congress soon responded by enacting an immigration law that brought about a virtual forty-year pause to digest, assimilate, and Americanize the diverse immigrant wave that had rolled in between 1890 and 1920.

Today, once again, it is impossible not to notice the conflicts generated by a new "hyphenated Americanism." In Los Angeles, two years ago, there was an anguishing afternoon in the Coliseum where the U.S. soccer team was playing Mexico. The Mexican-American crowd showered the U.S. team with water bombs, beer bottles and trash. The Star Spangled Banner was hooted and jeered. A small contingent of fans of the American team had garbage hurled at them. The American players later said that they were better received in Mexico City than in their own country.

Last summer, El Cenizo, a small town in south Texas, adopted Spanish as its official language. All town documents are now to be written, and all town business conducted, in Spanish. Any official who cooperates with U.S. immigration authorities was warned he or she would be fired. To this day, Governor Bush is reluctant to speak out on this de facto secession of a tiny Texas town to Mexico.

Voting in referendums that play a growing part in the politics of California is now breaking down sharply on ethnic lines. Hispanic voters opposed Proposition 187 to cut off welfare to illegal aliens, and they rallied against it under Mexican flags. They voted heavily in favor of quotas and ethnic preferences in the 1996 California Civil Rights Initiative, and, again, to keep bilingual education in 1998. These votes suggest that in the California of the future, when Mexican-American voting power catches up with Mexican-American population, any bid to end racial quotas by referendum will fail. A majority of the state's most populous immigrant group now appears to favor set-asides and separate language programs, rather than to be assimilated into the American mainstream.

The list of troubling signs can be extended. One may see them in the Wen Ho Lee nuclear secrets case, as many Chinese-Americans immediately concluded the United States was prosecuting Mr. Lee for racist reasons.

If we want to assimilate new immigrants ... we must slow down the pace of immigration.

Regrettably, a cultural Marxism called political correctness is taking root that makes it impossible to discuss immigration in any but the most glowing terms. In New York City billboards that made the simple point that immigration increases crowding and that polls show most Americans want immigration rates reduced were forced down under circumstances that came very close to government-sponsored censorship. The land of the free is becoming intolerant of some kinds of political dissent.

Sociologist William Frey has documented an out-migration of black and white Americans from California, some of them seeking better labor market conditions, others in search of a society like the one they grew up in. In California and other high immigration states, one also sees the rise of gated communities where the rich close themselves off from the society their own policies produce.

I don't want to overstate the negatives. But in too many cases the American Melting Pot has been reduced to a simmer. At present rates, mass immigration reinforces ethnic subcultures, reduces the incentives of newcomers to learn English; and extends the life of linguistic ghettos that might otherwise be melded into the great American mainstream. If we want to assimilate new immigrants—and we have no choice if we are remain one nation—we must slow down the pace of immigration.

Whatever its shortcomings, the United States has done far better at alleviating poverty than most countries. But an America that begins to think of itself as made up of disparate peoples will find social progress far more difficult. It is far easier to look the other way when the person who needs help does not speak the same language, or share a common culture or common history.

Americans who feel it natural and right that their taxes support the generation that fought World War II—will they feel the same way about those from Fukien Province or Zanzibar? If America continues on its present course, it could rapidly become a country with no common language, no common culture, no common memory and no common identity. And that country will find itself very short of the social cohesion that makes compassion possible.

None of us are true universalists: we feel responsibility for others because we share with them common bonds—common history and a common fate. When these are gone, this country will be a far harsher place.

That is why I am proposing immigration reform to make it possible to fully assimilate the 30 million immigrants who have arrived in the last thirty years. As President, I will ask Congress to reduce new entry visas to 300,000 a year, which is enough to admit immediate family members of new citizens, with plenty of room for many thousands with the special talents or skills our society needs. If after several years, it becomes plain that the United States needs more immigrants because of labor shortages, it should implement a point system similar to that of Canada and Australia, and allocate visas on a scale which takes into account education, knowledge of English, job skills, age, and relatives in the United States.

I will also make the control of illegal immigration a national priority. Recent reports of thousands of illegals streaming across the border into Arizona, and the sinister and cruel methods used to smuggle people by ship into the United States, demand that we regain control of our borders. For a country that cannot control its borders isn't fully sovereign; indeed, it is not even a country anymore.

Without these reforms, America will begin a rapid drift into uncharted waters. We shall become a country with a dying culture and deepening divisions along the lines of race, class, income and language. We shall lose for our children and for the children of the 30 million who have come here since 1970 the last best hope of earth. We will betray them all—by denying them the great and good country we were privileged to grow in. We just can't do that.

With immigration at the reduced rate I recommend, America will still be a nation of immigrants. We will still have the benefit of a large, steady stream of people from all over the world whose life dream is to be like us—Americans. But, with this reform, America will become again a country engaged in the mighty work of assimilation, of shaping new Americans, a proud land where newcomers give up their hyphens, the great American melting pot does its work again, and scores of thousands of immigrant families annually ascend from poverty into the bosom of Middle America to live the American dream.

Diversity: A Spirit of Community[3]

Albert C. Yates

President, Colorado State University, and Chancellor, Colorado State University System, 1990– ; B.S. magna cum laude in chemistry and mathematics, Memphis State University, 1965; Ph.D. in theoretical chemical physics, Indiana University at Bloomington, 1968; associate professor of chemistry, Indiana University, 1969–74; associate university dean for graduate education and research, University of Cincinnati, 1974–76; vice president and university dean for graduate studies and research, University of Cincinnati, 1977; executive vice president and provost, Washington State University in Pullman, 1982–90; distinguished alumnus, Memphis State University; University of Cincinnati Award for Excellence; Urban League of Metropolitan Denver Recognition Award for encouragement and support of the educational aspirations of Denver's minority students.

Editors' introduction: President Albert C. Yates spoke at a Black History Month reception at Colorado State University honoring his distinguished service to that institution. President Yates asked that we "reach out to those who suffer unseen and unloved."

Albert C. Yates' speech: Good afternoon and thank you for this wonderful tribute! I can think of nothing that would mean more to me than this—acknowledgment by you, the students of Colorado State University, that you appreciate and value what this institution has meant to you and the difference it has made in your lives.

As well, I would also like to thank you for the difference *you've* made in the life of this University—particularly those among you who have worked so hard to plan this year's Black History Month celebration. Your efforts have simply been extraordinary! By reaching out to share your programs and experiences with the larger campus, you have truly demonstrated the spirit of community and unity that makes Black History Month such an important event for this University.

Still, every month should be "Cultural Awareness Month." Each day should be a day when all among us—black and white and all in-between—should open their doors and windows to others so that we may all share the richness of cultural diversity.

---

3. Delivered in Fort Collins, Colorado, on February 28, 2001, at 2 p.m. Reprinted with permission of Albert C. Yates.

We live in a difficult time—a time of disturbing trends. In recent years, we have seen a resurgence of global racism; rampant violence in our cities; the hopelessness and despair of too many of our children; the explosive growth of a kind of an "in your face" mentality that makes rudeness and incivility accepted, even glorified traits; and so on. Sadly, we have even seen this behavior emerging too often on our college campuses, where people traditionally have been expected to model the very finest sort of human interaction.

It was in this context I thought about what I might say to you today. Over the past decade I've made hundreds of speeches covering a wide range of topics and concerns, including diversity, racism, multiculturalism, affirmative action and more. And as we end Black History month, what thoughts do we take with us? What imperatives bind and propel us?

As I have read and reread my writings of recent years, I offer two imperatives I hope you will embrace:

1. Leave no one behind; everyone deserves and, at times needs a helping hand.
2. All of our children, no matter their circumstances, should be seen and touched; they should all be given the substance of dreams of a better time and a better life, and the ability to live lives of dignity.

Please allow me to explain why these imperatives are important to me. And so I want to read a few paragraphs from two essays I wrote some years ago:

> Here's a list of a few names of high school friends from a world that now seems very far away:
>
> Jimmy Lacey.
>
> Three brothers—Junior, Herschel and Lloyd.
>
> Eight-ball.
>
> Honey.
>
> It seems we all had nicknames.

These names won't mean anything to you. They're the names of friends from times long since passed—young men who grew up with me in the black ghettos of Memphis, Tennessee. They were bright and energetic, creative minds and quick wits, ingenious negotiators—as well they had to be; they were people of great talent and vitality. And in those early years, their approval and companionship meant far more to me than that of my own family. In some ways—for that brief span of time in which life changes so dramatically from the games of children to the struggles of adulthood—this was my family.

Jimmy Lacey is dead now—his life snuffed out for some senseless reason like so many I've known. Junior, too, is gone, violently killed along with the rest of his family—a wife and small children. His brother Herschel drank himself into oblivion, and the youngest of the brothers, Lloyd, is imprisoned for life. And the doors closed on Eightball and Honey long, long ago. Like so many people born and raised in forgotten places, they were forgotten and left behind by a world that never seemed to have much use for them.

These names, these faces, haunt me. We were children together, we dreamed together. But somehow, some way, I was able to break the cycle of despair and build a life beyond the world into which I was born. They weren't. And there are few days when I don't hear that question—why me?—teasing at the corners of my mind.

We were in tough times together. I was no smarter, certainly no more virtuous, often less ambitious and resourceful—I could see then—as now—no visible advantage. So, again, why me? Over the years I've resigned myself to a simple and distressing conclusion: I was lucky. I had people who believed in me, who supported me, and who gave me the courage and the strength to pursue an education—people, for reasons often unknown to me, who extended a helping hand. The opportunity to pursue a useful and fulfilling life should not rest with the roll of the dice.

> *The opportunity to pursue a useful and fulfilling life should not rest with the roll of the dice.*

Here's my second story: I grew up in the Old South, in Memphis, Tennessee, during the times of segregated buses and movie theaters, public washrooms and lunch counters. One summer, when I was fourteen or fifteen years old, I drove a car for an old Jewish man who sold shoes to small-town general stores in rural areas. After a short while, the pattern of our relationship was set. I would arrive at his place early enough to begin the day at 6:30 a.m. And our weekly trek would take us through the hills of Tennessee; the flat, dusty roads of rural Arkansas; and the backwoods and bayous of Mississippi—returning to Memphis each evening around 7 p.m.

We spent long days together, talking about all manner of things, and even grew to be friends—of a sort. I had never been close to anyone white before and came with no knowledge of the Holocaust or of the historical persecution of Jews. I learned much that summer about racial and ethnic differences, about the politics of race; I began, too, to get a glimpse of the pervasiveness and the complexity of racism and bigotry—in subtle and not-so-subtle terms. But I learned much more, far more, no doubt, than my companion realized. Through this old man's eyes, I began to discover a world that had been denied to me. And through these and similar experiences, the substance of my own dreams was formed.

But the story doesn't end here. On those long, dusty roads, we sat as equals on the front seat of that old car, living and reliving our worlds, confident in our relationship but aware of our respective status. And as we approached each small town, we would go through our silent ritual: I would pull over to the side of the road; he would then take up his place in the back seat of the car; and later, I would gather the suitcases of shoe samples and assume my place, robot-like, used and useful, but unseen and unheard.

This experience was made clearer to me years later, as I read Ralph Ellison's *Invisible Man*; some of you will remember the prologue, which began in this way.

> I am an invisible man. No, I am not a spook like those who haunted Edgar Allan Poe; nor am I one of your Hollywood-movie ectoplasms. I am a man of substance, of flesh and bone, fiber and liquids—and I might even be said to possess a mind. I am invisible, understand, simply because people refuse to see me. Like the bodiless heads you see sometimes in circus sideshows, it is as though I have been surrounded by mirrors of hard, distorting glass. When they approach me, they see only my surroundings, themselves, or figments of their imagination—indeed, everything and anything except me.

And so, I have taken from these experiences a hope and a resolve that the generations to follow will never have to bear that pain. That same resolve of years ago directs my path today. At CSU, much remains for us to do:

- We must adopt a new and pervasive attitude about the relationship and connections among us.

- We must find new ways to celebrate our differences while cultivating and emphasizing the "samenesses" that unify and strengthen us as a nation and a people—remembering that our similarities are far greater in number than are our differences.

- We must continue to give special attention to the cultural and social needs of all students—but especially students of color who form an often unprotected minority. And we must find ways to do this without incurring anger, retaliation and backlash—and we can.

- Perhaps most important, we must resurrect the notion that universities play a critical role in developing human potential and serving as agents of positive social change. Students come to college, in large measure, unshaped and uncertain. Just as we expect a kindergarten teacher to educate young children in simple rules that teach discipline and good behavior—say "please" and "thank you," don't cut in line, respect other's belongings—we should expect college professors to help students achieve understanding at a higher level of the finest attributes of a civilized society: the ability to act fairly, reason plainly, behave honestly and accept responsibility for actions taken.

If we can do these things throughout our society, our future will be secure. If we can do these things, we can lessen the anger, fear and mistrust that make enemies of too many of us. But to make such changes will require the commitment and energy of each and every one of us.

I want to thank you again for making this day so very special, but I end in a request. I ask that you strive always to make a difference in this world, that you reach out to those who suffer unseen and unloved, that you will find ways to give all our children a chance to dream, and that you dedicate your passion and your energy to building a world in which all people have a chance to live life with dignity.

Thank you!

There Are Giants in Our Midst[4]

Steven J. Lebow

Senior Rabbi, Temple Kol Emeth, Atlanta, 1986– ; born Ft. Lauderdale, FL, March 18, 1955; honors graduate, Kenyon College; Hebrew Union College (M.A); Jewish Institute of Religion (Rabbinical ordination), 1983; Assistant Rabbi, Temple Sinai, New Orleans, Louisiana, 1983–86; Adjunct Professor, American History, University of New Orleans, 1983–86; Clergyman of the Year, National Conference of Christians and Jews, 1993; Social Action Award of the Union of American Hebrew Congregations, 1994; Social Justice Citation by Clergy and Laity Concerned, 1995; Courage Award, Cobb Citizens Coalition, 1996; Freedom and Justice Award by the Metropolitan Community Churches of America, 1998; has authored articles and speeches in The American Rabbi, The Jewish Post and Opinion, *and* The Christian Science Monitor.

Editors' introduction: Rabbi Steven J. Lebow addressed some 2,500 persons, including several hundred graduating seniors of Walton High School, Marietta, Georgia, their families and friends, and local clergy and dignitaries. This address was originally intended to be given at Mt. Bethel United Methodist Church, in Marietta, but the invitation was rescinded because the church's pastor felt uncomfortable with a non-Christian delivering a message from his pulpit. When word reached the public that he had been "dis-invited," the media coverage lasted close to two months. The Baccalaureate Committee eventually reinstated the invitation, and Rabbi Lebow spoke in the Cobb Civic Center. Rabbi Lebow explained that he intended his speech "to reach across religious boundaries and to stress our common values as Americans, living and working in a free and democratic society." Portions of the speech were carried on CNN, the major networks, and all local Atlanta TV stations. The address was printed in its entirety by the *Atlanta Journal-Constitution*.

Steven J. Lebow's speech: To you the graduates, the families, the faculty, the administration and the guests of the Walton High School . . .

From where I stand to where you are, I reach out my hands to each one of you. To the Baptist and to the Methodist, to the Episcopalian and to the Roman Catholic, to the Lutheran and to the Presbyterian—I reach out my hands in friendship and in fellowship to you.

---

4. Delivered in Marietta, Georgia, on May 22, 2001, at 7 p.m. Reprinted with permission of Rabbi Steven J. Lebow.

From where I stand, to where you are, to the Latter Day Saints and to the Adventists, to the Jehovah's Witnesses and to the Greek Orthodox, to the assemblies of God and to the Church of Christ—I reach out my hands to you.

From where I stand, to where you are, to Walton High School and to all its students—to the Sunni and the Shi'ite Muslim, to the Hindu and to the Jain, to the Budhist and the Shinto, to the Bahai and to the Sikh—*from where I stand to where you are*—I reach out my hands in friendship to you tonight.

I come here tonight as an American and as a Jew and I am humbled that you would honor me, and honor my fellow Jews, by asking that I would share a message with you tonight. I am grateful to my wife, Madeline, for her unfailing support and (I thank Monsignor Patrick Bishop for his wise counsel).

And tonight I ask for God's blessing, as I choose to concentrate, not on the things which can divide us as a community, but on the tremendous values which can bring us together. Tonight I choose to meditate on the awesome privilege of being an American and I choose to take the few minutes that you have given me to remind us all that *there are giants in our midst.*

We live in a media driven society, in which the worst news, the sickest individuals, and the bloodiest tragedies usually make the front page. The murderers, the degenerates and the degraded are impressed upon our consciousness moment after moment, and we lose sight of the truly good and decent human beings whose mundane and prosaic actions make this a better world every day.

My friends, *there are giants in our midst.* They don't ask for our thanks. They don't ask for our tributes, and they don't ask for our attention. But tonight I'm going to take a moment to single them out, because learning to give thanks to others, and to acknowledge true service is part of our need to come together now, as one holy and one complete community.

There are giants in our midst. Right now there are several hundred thousand people who wear the uniforms of the United States military. You don't know their names, you'll probably never meet them and if I hadn't stopped to tell you about them tonight you might never have thought about them.

The men and women of the U.S. military often serve long and lonely hours in faraway and desolate places. They do it for too little pay and for no real recognition. And because they do what they do this is a freer world in which to live, and it is a better world and it is a safer world.

People who serve in the U.S. military made it possible for you to live freely in Cobb County this year. And people who serve in the military made it possible, in a very real sense for me to be your speaker tonight, as well.

So look at me now and realize exactly what I am and what I represent. I am the descendant of European Jews, the people who were targeted for complete extinction by Hitler and his allies.

And if it were not for the bravery of the U.S. military I would not be here tonight. I don't ever forget that my family owes a debt to the United States, to my country, and to its military. And I don't ever take my freedom or my life for granted, nor should you.

People who serve in the U.S. military are everyday heroes and they don't ask to be acknowledged, but tonight I am going to do just that. So please bear with me, and don't be embarrassed. But if you are a veteran of any of the military services or if you are on active duty or in the Reserves, please stand now and let us acknowledge you and your contributions to our democracy . . .

There are giants in our midst and our lives in a very real sense depend on what they do for us each and every day.

There are those who serve in law enforcement, those who put on a badge everyday. That badge can make them a target, at any time. Police officers are my heroes.

> **There are giants in our midst *and our lives in a very real sense depend on what they do for us each and every day.***

There are firemen and EMTs who leap from fire trucks and ambulances and who crouch over burning cars and twisted metal—they're my heroes. They do a tough job under incredible pressure. Somebody you know, or somebody you love, may be in an accident one day. And if that person survives then it will be because an unnamed and unthanked fireman or EMT brought that person back to life. Firemen and EMTs are my heroes, too. *There are giants in our midst.*

You know I am a Rabbi, a clergyman, and I spend half my life in hospitals, as I comfort the families of the sick or the dying. And day in and day out, I get a chance to watch the people who truly minister to the sick. I watch the nurses who come into our hospital rooms, they change our dressings, they bandage our wounds, they check our IVs. And they served where most of us could not stand. Nurses are my heroes, too.

So if you're a law enforcement officer of any kind, if you're a fireman or an EMT, if you're a nurse of any kind, won't you please rise now and just give us a chance, one chance in our lives to acknowledge *that there are giants in our midst?* Please rise now—

There is a group who is here tonight who has been an awesome contributor to your lives. And you probably don't even know how much you owe them, and you may not know it for another 20 or 30 years, until you stand where I have stood tonight.

If you are a Walton High School senior, this group of people has worked with you, they have struggled with you, they have urged you on, and they have encouraged you in all of your endeavors.

If you needed a little extra help with a quiz, maybe one of them was there for you. If you don't understand a math problem or a formula in science, then one of these people tried to pass that knowledge along to you. And if you were an athlete, during the last 4 years, then one of these people spent hours with you, in the weight room or on the football field, running drills on the basketball court or helping you perfect your serve in tennis. They were there at six in the morning when you swam laps in the pool, or at six in the night when you ran wind sprints, or practiced your gold swing, or your cheerleading. And they have experienced the thrill of victory with you and they have suffered the agony of defeat with you and if they are not your heroes, then they ought to be.

There are giants in our midst—because there are people here tonight who taught you how to write a topic sentence, who taught you how to hold your musical instruments, who taught you how to memorize the periodic table. And sadly enough, it probably will not be until long after they are dead and gone that you will realize how much they gave to you and to your fellow classmates.

You see, when you have stood where I have stood, then you know that we sometimes forget to thank our teachers and our coaches, our counselors and our administrators. But I'm not going to let you forget tonight. I'm going to remind you to thank all those who assisted in your education.

So bear with me one more time. And if you are a Walton High School teacher, or coach, if you are an administrator, an employee, or a counselor at Walton High School, in fact if you are anybody's teacher anywhere, please rise now, because you're one of my heroes—and let us all acknowledge the awesome things that you have done with your life, by dedicating it to teaching.

So now we come to the end of my list of common people who do uncommon things, ordinary people who do extra-ordinary things. I am speaking now of the people that you have sometimes forgotten to thank, the people who were always there for you.

They are the people who bought you your first pair of shoes, when you were 3 months old. They dressed you until you were about 4 years old, when you were infants you threw up on their shoulders and when you were toddlers they wiped your little tushes and they never once asked that you should thank them.

When you were 6 they taught you how to ride a bike or how to throw a ball. And when you had your first fever, they stayed up all night with you, they were proud of you when you brought home your first good grade, and they were happy when you went to your first dance. And now tonight, you should forgive them if they are maybe more than just a little bit sad, as you begin to take the next steps forward in your lives.

Mark Twain once said, "When I was 18 I was convinced that my father was the stupidest man that I had ever met in my life and when I turned 21 I was amazed at how much the old man had learned in just three short years . . ."

So when you come to stand where I must stand, when you yourselves are parents, then at last you will see how difficult a task it is. No one of us ever gets being a parent just right, and all of us who are parents just try to do the best that we can, each and every day.

Maybe someday, if your hearts are open to the reality of life, when you understand that life is just about showing up and doing your job, then you will come to see that your parents and your grandparents were the greatest heroes that you ever knew.

So now, I would like to turn to you, to the parents and the grandparents of the Walton High School seniors. And I would like to ask the parents and grandparents to rise now. And I would like to let their children applaud and then let the children acknowledge that *there are indeed giants in our midst.*

In closing, I know that you are expecting me to try to find some meaning in the whole controversy that preceded tonight's baccalaureate service. So let me conclude by offering one level of meaning within the context of finding our heroes.

Do you want to know who the true heroes were of this whole controversy? Do you want to know who my heroes are?

John Flatt, your principal is my hero. Because he had to guide you through what was a wrenching time he was the very definition of grace under pressure. Grace under pressure.

John Flatt is one of my heroes.

Clair Stanfill, Pat Guliani and Flo Leach, and thirty members of your baccalaureate committee are my heroes. They volunteered for what they thought would be a typical boring service. But history unraveled in a different way and so they had to struggle and to prevail.

Julia Levy, a Walton High School senior, is also one of my unsung heroes. Because she didn't know when she suggested that I be your speaker tonight that it would kick off a media firestorm. You know, she's just an 18-year-old kid. All she wanted to do this spring was to go to the prom, get a summer job and then go off to college.

But sometimes, Julia, history has different things in mind for us than we have for ourselves. We are thrown into the fire and we have to call upon the resources that we never knew we had. Julia Levy is one of my heroes. Because she has been through the fire and she has lived to tell the tale.

Heroes are ordinary people who do extraordinary things. They show up and they do the jobs that they felt called to do. And so, I have two final suggestions for you, they are the heroes of the debate that emerged before this baccalaureate service could occur.

One is a reporter and the other is a protestant minister and they both did their jobs, exactly as they were supposed to do, in a free and democratic society.

Don Fernandez is the 31-year-old reporter who first reported on the Walton Baccalaureate story. And during the uproar this past

---

> *Heroes are ordinary people who do extraordinary things. They show up and they do the jobs that they felt called to do.*

---

spring I am sure that there were many who wished that Don and his colleagues from the media would just go away. I am reasonably sure that people wanted the media to go away, because if I recall, I was one of them.

But in retrospect, I have come to see that the media, flawed as it may be, must also play its part in a free and open society.

Don Fernandez and his colleagues in the media represent one of the greatest institutions that we have here in America; a free and unfettered press. The media plays a necessary role in any healthy democracy.

Just as America needs our military and our law enforcement, so too we need a media free to report on events, even when we disagree with their interpretations. And when we understand what Don Fernandez and all the media represent, then we will understand, why they, too, are the heroes of our democracy. They do a necessary job, for which they are often unpopular, but without a free press, this would not be the country that it is.

You see, the heroes of democracy, the true American heroes, are often simple men and women who live for higher values and ideals. They are soldiers and police, firemen and EMTs, nurses and teachers, your parents and your grandparents, the media and the ministry.

So fittingly, my final hero of our democracy is the Rev. Randy Mickler, of Mt. Bethel United Methodist Church. Now, I know that you might think that it is odd for me to say that Randy is a hero, since it must seem that he and I are on different sides of the issue.

But when you stand where I have stood, then you come to see that reasonable people can and do disagree. Good and decent people can disagree and still respect each other for the passion and the strength of their convictions.

This is America, and in America the Constitution and the Bill of Rights guarantee our basic freedoms; the freedom of religion, the freedom of speech and the freedom of association.

This is America, and in America we don't practice genocide or holy wars. We don't' kill each other over religious differences.

As Americans we enter into a sacred and holy compact, in which we defend each other's right to express our opinions, even when we might choose to disagree with those opinions.

This is America, and in America the Reverend Micklers and the Rabbi Lebows can disagree one month about what constitutes a baccalaureate service, and in the next month we can stand side by side and build a house for Habitat for Humanity—just as we will begin doing tomorrow afternoon, at 1 p.m.

Because you see, this is America, and in America the Reverend Micklers and the Rabbi Lebows don't have to agree on everything. In America we are of different faiths, different races, and different national and ethnic origins.

This is our struggle, but it is also our strength.

This is America and as Americans we enter into a sacred and holy compact, in which we defend each other's right to express our opinions, even when we might choose to disagree with those opinions.

Randy Mickler is a hero, because each and every day he simply tries to serve the Lord, and from time to time his faith will lead him to take unpopular stands.

But this is America. That's what Pastor Mickler is allowed to do. In fact, that's what he is supposed to do! I defend the positions that Pastor Mickler took, because he took them out of his deep and honest convictions as a Christian and as the pastor of his church. So if you want to attack Christians or Pastor Mickler or his church, then you will have to go straight through me.

As a Jew and as an American I will defend him, because all of us are bound up in this great and holy experiment that we call democracy and all of us are part of an agreement to preserve, protect and defend the freedom of the other guy.

So now do you get it? Now do you see what your senior year was all about?

You see, in many ways your senior year was a teachable moment, it was a kind of political science seminar, if you will, in which you got to see exactly how people need to function in a free and democratic society.

This past spring students and parents at Walton High School had vastly different opinions and completely different interpretations about what could and what should happen at tonight's baccalaureate.

At first, our differences drove us apart and we all talked so loudly that none of us could hear what the other guy was saying.

But after all the interviews were over and after all the press conferences were held. After all the sermons were given, and after all the editorials were written, after all the harsh words that could have driven us apart were said, we were all left with the only reality that we all have to live with.

You see—I'm just one small man on a very large stage but I came here tonight to offer you the biggest message that I know.

This is America. This is a country where we respect each other's differences.

This is America—In our country we defend each other's differences.

The greatest American of the twentieth century was Dr. Martin Luther King, and Dr. King used to teach *that in spite of and because of* our differences we must come to think of ourselves as the "Beloved Community." There are only two choices, Dr. King once taught, it's either chaos or community.

So this is my simple message to you, the graduates of Walton High School.

From where I stand to where you are.

Look around you tonight before you leave this place. And recognize within it if you will—

For yours was the privilege to have these men and women as your teachers.

Yours was the blessing to call these families your own.

Yours was the honor to call yourselves American.

And yours is now the opportunity to become God's highest blessing, in these and coming years.

To become the giants in our midst.

So God bless you all tonight, and God bless America.

V. Energy

Remarks at the Fifth Annual Green Power Marketing Conference[1]

Kathleen B. Hogan

Director, Climate Protection Partnerships Division of the U.S. Environmental Protection Agency, 1989– ; born New Haven, CT, August 10, 1957; graduate of Bucknell University; Ph.D., Whiting School of Engineering, Johns Hopkins University; Water Resources Systems Engineer for Interstate Commission on Potomac River Basin, 1983–87; Senior Associate at ICF Consulting, 1987–89; author of papers and reports showing cost-effective approaches for reducing emissions of greenhouse gases.

Editors' introduction: The mission of the U.S. Environmental Protection Agency (EPA) is to protect human health and to safeguard the natural environment—air, water, and land—upon which life depends. Director Kathleen B. Hogan addressed some 200 clean energy industry representatives attending the Fifth Annual Green Power Marketing Conference sponsored by the U.S. Department of Energy. She envisioned "a transition away from a utility system based on fossil fuels to one based on clean energy sources."

Kathleen B. Hogan's speech: Good morning. EPA and the green power industry are natural allies in environmental protection, so I appreciate the opportunity to be with you.

I would like to accomplish three things this morning in my remarks. First, I want to make it clear that EPA understands the environmental benefits that can be delivered from clean energy and green power. Second, I would like to provide you with an update on recent events at EPA which mean that EPA will be increasing its role in the green power area. And third, I would like to share with you our general approach for moving forward.

So the facts on the U.S. electric industry:

- The electricity industry is one of the nation's largest sources of pollution.

- This year, U.S. electricity generators will produce an estimated 589 million metric tons of carbon, over one-third of total U.S. energy-related carbon emissions; an estimated 11.7 million tons of sulfur dioxide emissions, almost two-thirds of the nation's

---

1. Delivered at Denver, Colorado, on August 7, 2000, at 11 a.m. Reprinted with permission of Kathleen B. Hogan.

total; and roughly 5 million tons of nitrogen oxide emissions, about one-fourth of the nation's total.

- These emissions contribute to health and environmental problems such as ground-level ozone, acid rain, fine particulate pollution, nitrogen deposition, and global climate change—one of the most pressing international environmental problems.

- The electricity industry is also the nation's largest source of mercury emissions. As was re-affirmed in a recent study by the National Academy of Sciences, mercury poses a significant health hazard.

- There is also an enormous amount of waste produced by the current U.S. power generation system. The amount of waste heat from our nation's power plants is greater than Japan's total energy use, including all of the energy needed to heat and cool its buildings, power its industrial operations and provide transportation.

- The efficiency of the electric system efficiency in the U.S. has not substantially improved since the 1960s

In short, our current, largely fossil-based, electricity generation system is inefficient and damaging to the environment. Let's look at global climate change for a moment:

- Scientists believe that if we continue on our current path of fossil-based energy use, we could see average temperatures rise 2 to 6 degrees F over the 21st century. Even at the low end, this means a rate of change that has not been seen for at least the last 10,000 years.

- This means major changes to our climates as we know them—more extreme weather events such as droughts and hurricanes. It means spread of warm climate diseases such as malaria and dengue fever as well as spread of warm climate crop diseases and pests.

- Enough is known that it is time to take action to address the risk of climate change.

- Many countries are trying with negotiation of the Kyoto Protocol—which has not been ratified by the U.S.—would require the nation to reduce its greenhouse gas emissions 7% below 1990 levels by 2010.

- While there is a great deal of debate about the Kyoto Protocol and whether it is too much too fast, it is clear that this problem is here to stay.

- This issue is not going away with the Clinton Administration or the next Administration or the next.

You Are an Important Part of the Solution

There are only a few ways to reduce our national greenhouse gas emissions in a smart way:

- One where I have tremendous experience is in reducing the wasteful use of energy in places where we as a country have been quite wasteful—in our homes, our buildings and some of our industries.

- Facts—the typical house causes more CO_2 in a year than a typical car; it takes more energy to support an employee at work for the day than for that employee to get to and from work; many homes and buildings can use 30% less energy through cost-effective investments in technology.

- With Energy Star we are having terrific success in reducing this waste: we have identified the reasons that energy efficient products and services have been hard to move in the marketplace; we have designed and implemented solutions; we have listened to partners across the country; we continue to evolve as the market changes; and we have had terrific success.

- Another way to address global climate change is through clean energy—that is to reduce the carbon emissions associated with the energy we need. Accelerating the supply of and the demand for clean energy is a key part of the solution.

- The timing for clean energy is good—the restructuring of the electricity industry which is sweeping the country provides an opportunity for change. And we have information that consumers are taking advantage of this opportunity. As you know, among consumers who have switched power providers, many have switched to green power—a trend which bodes well for the future. If enough government entities, businesses, organizations and consumers switch to green power, the environmental benefits would be tremendous.

- For example, the Green Power Market Development Group has announced a goal of 1000 MW of new green power capacity, which could translate into the installation of over a thousand new wind turbines. We hope to persuade other companies to take similar actions to spur development of the clean energy market.

- Here, I have an announcement—EPA is creating a new staff within my Division that will focus on energy supply issues, including green power. I'd like to tell you about a few green power-related activities at EPA, as well as how this new staff will be approaching their work.

First, we at EPA are leading by example. Last summer, EPA bought power generated from renewable sources for our Richmond, California, laboratory, making EPA the first federal agency to buy 100 percent green power. EPA has also purchased blocks of wind power for a facility we have in Golden, Colorado. We are also exploring opportunities to purchase green power for many more of EPA's facilities nationwide.

EPA and DOE are committed to doubling CHP capacity by 2010. We've established a Energy Star CHP Award to build a higher profile and recognition for the best performing of the CHP family of technologies. And we're committed to working with our stakeholders to better understand how our regulations can stimulate deployment of CHP technologies.

We are starting to think about how we can leverage the clean air regulatory structure to accelerate deployment of renewable energy. We have started working with States in thinking about how renewable energy could play a role in helping them to meet their air quality attainment goals. We are also building output based emissions allocations into new air quality regulations which will provide utilities with an additional incentive to move towards cleaner generation sources.

We are continuing to provide technical assistance in the development of new landfill gas to energy projects.

We are developing new information tools. To educate people about the environmental implications of their energy choices, we have developed a national Public Service Announcement campaign which helps consumers understand that when they flip a switch, they are in effect turning on a smokestack. The TV spot features a man trying to start a television by pulling a starter cord as if it were a smoke-spewing gas-powered lawnmower. The spot is currently playing in 46 different markets, and it has played over 30,000 times nationwide.

We are continuing to develop an important information database on the emissions of air pollution associated with power plants around the country—known as E-GRID. As electric industry restructuring continues to happen, we expect that E-GRID will encourage the development of cleaner electricity resources by helping consumers to be better informed about the sources of their electricity. Several states are already using E-GRID as a data source for information disclosure by electricity providers. And E-GRID can help states that are adopting innovative output-based approaches to regulating emissions.

We have strong expertise in all of these areas and will be working to put together an action plan over the fall that we can deliver on and which we believe will deliver substantial environmental benefit.

We're pleased that in the President's latest budget request, the Administration is requesting a $124 million increase in 2001 funding for EPA's climate change technology programs. That represents a 120% increase over 2000 enacted levels.

Over the next decade, we estimate this increase will deliver $35 billion in energy savings to families and businesses; and 850,000 tons of NO_2 emissions reductions.

We hope to use this increased funding to build consumer awareness around the Energy Star Label to enhance the demand for energy efficiency, and to expand our clean power initiatives. Again, using clean power is the logical extension of the work we have been doing to spur new technologies into the marketplace to prevent pollution. Of course there's often a difference between what the President proposes and what becomes law. But I believe this signals that our partnership with DOE to promote energy efficiency and spur new technologies remains strong, and that our Administration is committed to continuing and expanding this work.

We may be at the beginning of a transition away from a utility system based on fossil fuels to one based on clean energy sources, and EPA has an interest in accelerating this transition. The changes currently underway in the electricity industry provide us with an opportunity to chart a new energy future—away from a system dominated by inefficient, fossil-fuel burning power plants, and towards a system of clean generation. We at EPA are just beginning new efforts in clean energy—and we look forward to working in partnership with you as we develop these efforts. There are a number of people from this group here with you—Kurt Johnson, Cynthia Cummis, and Tom Kerr. Please search them out and share your thoughts. I again thank you for the opportunity to be with you this morning.

Remarks on California Electricity Event[2]

Bill Richardson

Secretary, United States Department of Energy, 1998–2000; born in Pasadena, CA, November 15, 1947; B.A., Tufts University, 1970; M.A., Fletcher School of Law and Diplomacy, MA, 1971; staff member, U.S. House of Representatives, 1971–72; member, Department of State, 1973–75; staff member, Senate Foreign Relations Committee, 1975–76; executive director, New Mexico State Democrat Committee, 1978; Democrat, U.S. House of Representatives, District 3, New Mexico, 1983–1997; committees in U.S. House of Representatives: Energy and Commerce, Subcommittee on Energy and Power, Subcommittee on Telecommunications and Finance, Interior and Insular Affairs, Energy and the Environment, Public Lands, Aging, and Intelligence; U.S. Ambassador to United Nations, 1997–98.

Editors' introduction: When the U.S. Senate confirmed Bill Richardson as Secretary of Energy, President Bill Clinton stated, "As a member of the U.S. Congress representing New Mexico, an energy-rich state that is home to two Department of Energy national laboratories, he has extensive firsthand experience on issues ranging from oil and gas deregulation to alternative energy, to ensuring strong environmental standards in energy development." With California's electrical power supplies running dangerously low, Secretary Richardson envisioned ways of reducing electricity consumption and developing existing resources.

Bill Richardson's speech: We're here today because California's electricity market has become dysfunctional. Since last summer, we've seen sky-high wholesale rates and tight supplies. More than once, the California Independent System Operator nearly imposed rolling blackouts throughout the state. In San Diego, residents and businesses saw their electric bills double almost overnight.

Some say government can't do anything to improve people's lives. I don't buy that. It's not our job to interfere with markets. But sometimes, when those markets are broken, we can work together to make a difference. This is one of those times. We can—and we must—act.

---

2. Delivered in Sacramento, California, on November 1, 2000.

Because of Governor Davis' leadership, and because of state legislators such as Dede Alpert and Susan Davis, the people of San Diego are no longer at the mercy of rates set by malfunctioning electric markets. The state is also working hard to deliver much-needed new electricity generation capacity without compromising its commitment to the environment. And through the California Energy Commission, the state is using energy efficiency and renewable resources to reduce rates and keep the lights on and air conditioners chilling during heat waves.

This is an issue that also calls for cooperation between California and the federal government. This past summer, the Clinton/Gore Administration took action:

- We generated more power at federal dams, through our power marketing administrations, to help California avoid blackouts. For instance, on one day in August, Bonneville provided an additional 1,000 megawatts to keep the lights on in California.

- We provided more than $2 million in emergency Low Income Home Energy Assistance Program funds to help deal with this crisis in San Diego; and

- Federal agencies cut electricity consumption at our facilities in California on days when power supplies were tight to prevent blackouts. This is no small thing—the federal government is the state's biggest energy consumer.

But more can and must be done. We need to help stabilize the electricity market in California. We need to help the state deal with supply shortages by increasing power supplies. And we need to improve energy efficiency. This will reduce costs for consumers, and reduce the need for additional power plants, thus reducing related pollution.

But Congress also needs to give the Federal Energy Regulatory Commission (FERC) added authority to keep generating companies from abusing their market power to profit at the expense of consumers. I met with Chairman Hoecker last Friday and told him that President Clinton and Vice President Gore are concerned about the situation here and that consumers need immediate relief.

We are still reviewing the FERC proposal released this morning. My initial impression is that it is a good start, but, as a party to the Commission's proceedings, the Energy Department will be pushing for FERC to act as aggressively as possible to protect consumers in California.

Congress also needs to take a serious look at Congressman Fillner's proposal to allow the Commission to order those companies that charge unreasonable rates to refund those overcharges back to consumers. Instead, the best the House of Representatives has done this year is simply pass a resolution that called on FERC to release a report five days earlier than originally scheduled.

Beyond the regulation of wholesale rates, there's more that needs to be done. So today, I'm announcing a series of initiatives the Clinton/Gore Administration is taking to ease the strain on the system and protect consumers in California and elsewhere:

- The Western Area Power Administration, an Energy Department agency that co-owns a major substation in Northern California, will provide $2 million to add a second transformer at the site. This will help California bring in much-needed power from the Pacific Northwest.

- The Energy Department will seek comments on proposed rules for utilities to follow to protect the reliability of the electric grid in California and elsewhere. The Administration and others have been pressing Congress to enact these much-needed rules to protect consumers. However, this bill has stalled. Therefore, we are going to try to do administratively what Congress failed to accomplish this year—establish mandatory reliability standards for electricity.

- I have directed the Western Area Power Administration and the Bonneville Power Administration to continue working with California to alleviate the problems of excess power produced by federal dams. For instance, I can report today that Bonneville's contract to provide low-cost power to Bay Area Rapid Transit will continue for many years to come; and

- The Energy Department will form a partnership with the State of California to ensure that our many energy efficiency and renewable energy programs and resources—more than $40 million worth this year in California alone—are put to use to help the state with its electricity problems.

We have formed a working group from our Seattle Regional Office, our Washington, D.C., headquarters and the National Laboratories to help coordinate these efforts.

And in Sacramento today, federal agency heads are meeting to identify ways we can ease electricity consumption in California, especially during times of high demand. Some of the participants are here with us today. The federal government is the state's single biggest energy user in the state. Our goal for next summer is to cut electricity use by ten percent in the more than 25,000 federal buildings in California.

We are working also to make major energy-consuming appliances more efficient. Earlier this month, the Energy Department proposed new standards for central air-conditioners and heat pumps, to use up to 30 percent less electricity. We've already set new standards for refrigerators, room air conditioners, and fluorescent lights, and they're already having an impact. When the Clinton-Gore Administration completes its term in January, standards we have set will save enough energy in the year 2010 to light every home in the country for two years. And by using less electricity, consumers will spend less money.

We need tax credits proposed by the Administration to encourage people to buy more of these efficient air conditioners. The California Energy Commission strongly supports this effort. I'm disappointed that Congress' tax bill failed to adopt these tax incentives.

In another action to save energy and money for consumers, we're awarding $500,000 in grants to the California Energy Commission to support programs that will make buildings in California more energy efficient. This, too, is no small thing—buildings in California account for approximately 8% of all building energy use in the U.S.

The Energy Department also has provided California with more than $3.7 million this year to help weatherize 3,081 low-income households in the state. We will be providing $4.2 million next year. This will help lower electricity bills for those who can least afford high prices. It is they who spend four times more than middle income consumers spend on energy as a percentage of income. Low-income consumers spend about 14 percent of their income on energy. In comparison, the average consumer spends only 3.5 percent.

And we are working with the state and local governments to help develop the tremendous renewable resources here, such as wind, solar, geothermal and biomass. For instance, we will be awarding $3 million in next year's budget for California wind projects. And we will provide $5.6 million for California geothermal projects, including $2 million to help increase energy production at the geysers in Napa Valley, the world's largest geothermal facility.

And this effort is nationwide. Yesterday, in Kansas City, I announced that the Energy Department and the Agriculture Department will together spend more than $250 million on biomass technology next year. And in the last two months, we have launched four different projects to accelerate research into bio-mass fuels from plants, sugars and other natural sources.

In these efforts, your federal government and the state of California are partners. And we look forward to continue working with Governor Davis and the others here today to help California lower its electricity prices, and to help keep the lights from going out. We have no choice—if we do not work together, we may end up sitting in the dark, alone. Thank you.

A National Energy Crisis Is upon Us[3]

Frank H. Murkowski

Republican United States Senator, Alaska, 1981– ; born in Seattle, WA, March 28, 1933; graduated Ketchikan High School; attended Santa Clara University; B.A. in economics, Seattle University, 1955; U.S. Coast Guard, 1955–57; National Bank of Alaska, 1966–67; Commissioner of Alaska Department of Economic Development, 1967–70; President of Alaska National Bank, Fairbanks, 1970–80; President of Alaska Bankers Association,1973; President, Alaska State Chamber of Commerce, 1977; U.S. Senate committees: chairman, Veterans Affairs, 1985–86; ranking member, Senate Intelligence Committee, 1991–92; chairman (1995–2001) and member (2001–), Committee on Energy and Natural Resources; member, Committees on Finance, Veterans' Affairs, and Indian Affairs; author of articles in Harvard Journal of Legislation, *2000.*

Editors' introduction: As elected officials, government appointees, and leaders from the private sector debated the availability, reliability, cost, and environmental impact of energy sources, Senator Frank H. Murkowski expressed his views to some 1,200 experts attending a summit sponsored by the U.S. Chamber of Commerce in that organization's auditorium. To remedy the "energy crisis," he and Senator John Breaux introduced in the U.S. Senate their National Energy Security Act of 2001, which he discussed in this speech. The speech was carried over C-SPAN. In response to the speech, the Senator received "some favorable letters."

Frank H. Murkowski's speech: Good day. First let me thank Tom Donohue, president of the U.S. Chamber of Commerce, for asking me to speak to you today.

My message to you today is simple, we are in the midst of an energy crisis in this country. Just look at the headlines of recent days.

From the *Washington Post*, "OPEC Cuts Oil Output," This is the second time this year that OPEC has reduced its oil production, bringing total OPEC production down by a combined 2.5 million barrels a day to date.

---

3. Delivered in Washington, D.C., on March 20, 2001, at 9:30 a.m. Reprinted with permission of Frank H. Murkowski.

From the *Wall Street Journal*, there is this story that says New York needs 8,600 megawatts of new power—a 25 percent increase— by 2005 or electricity prices will go up and blackouts could occur in New York City.

From California papers, yesterday there were rolling blackouts throughout the state affecting 675,000 homes. The blackouts occurred partially because of a lack of electricity available for import from the Pacific Northwest.

Secretary of Energy Spencer Abraham in his remarks suggested that the energy crisis sweeping the nation should shock the political system into action. He further stated that a failure to meet the challenge threatens our national security, our economic prosperity and will affect the way we live our lives.

Unfortunately there is not yet a sense of national crisis, but that could change by later this summer if blackouts continue in California and gasoline and natural gas prices continue to soar.

National Energy Legislation

Last month I and Senator John Breaux in a bipartisan manner introduced the National Energy Security Act of 2001. It is 303 pages long and all anyone in the press ever mentions is the section involving opening of the Arctic National Wildlife Refuge's (ANWRs) coastal plain to oil and gas development. I want to use this appearance to tell you about what's in the rest of the bill.

Our national energy strategy is far more than "just ANWR."

It contains new programs and incentives to help find, develop, deliver and conserve all our domestic energy resources.

It expands production of conventional sources of energy—coal, oil, natural gas, and nuclear to provide energy for continued economic growth.

And we improve the environmental quality of these fuels by:

1. Investing in advanced research and development programs, and
2. Providing tax incentives for deployment of new, cleaner, more efficient technologies.

We encourage new investment in energy infrastructure—transmission lines, natural gas pipelines, and drilling equipment.

And we take steps to ensure the reliability of the nation's electric power supply, so critical to today's "New Economy."

We also provide new programs and incentives to expand the supply of renewable energy at home and alternative fuels in your car.

A robust domestic energy industry—both fossil and renewable— also helps to keep energy prices stable and affordable. And that's good for business, and it's good for consumers.

More Than Just Supply

But our legislation is not only about supply—as some would have you think. We also focus on using energy more efficiently.

Our legislation expands funding for weatherization and the LIHEAP (Low-Income Heating and Energy Assistance) programs. We move to lower the monthly energy bills and protect consumers and low-income families from the effects of higher prices.

We also encourage state and regional energy conservation programs to minimize the effects of regional shortages in supply—like the kinds of problems we've seen in California.

This legislation includes several new incentives to conserve energy resources and improve efficiency (appliances, homes and vehicles).

Finally, we provide new incentives for emerging distributed energy and combined heat and power technologies.

And most importantly, we provide no incentives for "Big Oil" as the media suggests. Our bill does not include ATM assistance (alternative tax provisions), only aid to tiny stripper well producers.

The legislation we have introduced is a first attempt to articulate the elements of a sound national energy strategy. Other elements that we must also address separately include: access issues, regulatory reform, nuclear waste and climate change concerns.

Senate Democrats are expected to introduce their own bill this week. Expect quite a bit of similarity between the two proposals.

We plan to hold numerous hearings to make the case for each aspect of our plan and consider options on the global impacts of the energy crisis. Our first hearing will be tomorrow, focusing on a general overview of U.S. energy trends and markets.

We expect that the Vice President's Energy Development Policy Group will make recommendations in May that we will use to further improve our bill and we are open to your suggestions and ideas as we go forward.

Some History

At no time in our history have we relied upon others for more of our energy supplies. Twenty years ago, the U.S imported just over one-third of the oil it consumed. Today, that has increased to 57 percent.

The Center for Strategic and International Studies (CSIS) predicts this trend will continue. They predict that by 2020, nearly one-half of estimated global oil demand will be supplied by countries with a high risk of instability.

We need only look to California for an example of what can happen, if we become too reliant on outside sources of energy.

In California electricity has had to be imported from out-of-state because there wasn't enough new generation to meet new demand.

There is clearly a parallel to domestic oil production, which has been in decline. Our increased reliance on foreign oil affects our foreign policy.

In 1991, we went into Kuwait to protect our access to foreign oil. In Operation Desert Storm some 148 Americans were killed, 467 wounded and 23 taken prisoner. Even now we continue to enforce "no-fly" zones over northern and southern Iraq. We have flown more than 234,000 sorties, which means that on 234,000 occasions we have put American lives at risk.

The ironic thing about our policy is that by effectively lifting sanctions against Saddam Hussein we are buying his oil, taking that oil and putting it into our airplanes, and then using that fuel to bomb him. Meanwhile Saddam is taking our cash to finance his repressive regime.

Please note that Iraq is our fastest growing source of imported oil. We have imported has much as 750,000 barrels a day from Iraq in the past year. And Saddam is ready to take an ever greater hold on the world oil market, often threatening to cut production if sanctions are not further reduced.

Aren't these policies compromising our national security?

We need only look to California for an example of what can happen, if we become too reliant on outside sources of energy.

The Effects of the Energy Crisis

The energy crisis is not just high oil prices and electricity shortages:

- Natural gas prices are double what they were last year. Some 56 million homes (50%) use natural gas for heating.

- U.S. refining capacity has dropped by 11 percent in the past 20 years as nearly half of America's refineries have closed (down to 155 from 315).

- Fewer new coal-fired electric power plants have come on line. Coal provides 52 percent of U.S. electricity. It is cheap and plentiful, but domestic fuel permits are hard to come by because of the new source review requirements.

- Nuclear power is vital for America as it provides 20 percent of our electricity. But because of concerns over waste, no new plants have come on line, and it will be hard to keep existing plants operating in the future without policy changes. That is especially ironic in a period of concern about greenhouse gases and climate change since nuclear energy emits, no carbon dioxide or other greenhouse gases.

- Hydroelectric plants are another source of "clean" electricity—emitting no greenhouse gases. Still we seldom license new plants and recently have even proposed removal of some dams.

The underlying problem is that production of energy—its supply—is not keeping pace with demand.

We have to use new technology to make these existing fuel sources cleaner and safer and we have to develop new technology, from fuel cells to new types of wind, solar and geothermal energy, to meet our booming energy demand.

The rapid growth of the Internet and the economic boom of the 1990s has led to significant increases in demand for energy.

The energy crisis threatens the growth of our economy. High oil prices could reduce U.S. economic growth by as much as 2 percent

---

> *The rapid growth of the Internet and the economic boom of the 1990s has led to significant increases in demand for energy.*

---

per year. Lost gross domestic product (GDP) could top $165 billion a year with 5.5 million fewer jobs in America.

The impacts on the American consumer already are clear: Higher energy prices means less economic growth and less prosperity for all.

The Need for ANWR

While we can't drill our way out of our energy crisis, we also can't conserve our way out. We need to both increase domestic energy sources, reduce our dependence on foreign sources and increase conservation and development of efficient, alternative energy sources if we are to preserve our economic and national security.

If we do nothing, by 2010, 30 supertankers each day will be required to visit American ports to deliver crude oil. Do we care where we get our oil? We certainly should care, especially those on the West Coast that predominately gain their oil from Alaska.

And that brings me to an Alaskan issue, ANWR. Geologists tell us the best place to look for oil in North America is along a tiny sliver of the Arctic coastal plain. The Arctic National Wildlife Refuge is 19 million acres in size—the size of South Carolina. In 1980, Congress set aside a tiny area, 1.5 million acres of the refuge, to be considered for future oil and gas exploration.

President Carter in signing the legislation establishing ANWR said the bill "strikes a balance between protecting areas of great beauty and value and allowing development of Alaska's vital oil and gas and mineral and timber resources . . . 95 percent of the potentially productive oil and mineral areas will be available for exploration or for drilling."

If ANWR is not open for development, that statement is certainly questionable. ANVWR oil reserves, which the U.S. Geological Survey estimates may contain 16 billion barrels of economically recoverable reserves, could yield a field the size of Prudhoe Bay—if not far bigger. It would be the biggest oil field we've discovered in the past 30 years. It could produce enough oil to replace imports from Saudi Arabia for 30 years or more.

Some in the Senate have threatened a filibuster to prevent Arctic development. That is the equivalent of fiddling while Rome burns. Some who oppose development won't even come to visit the area and see for themselves the new technology that exists to allow oil development.

And the key is that new technology does exist to do it safely with a much smaller footprint and with less environmental disturbance than ever before.

Today we have ice roads and directional drilling that will reduce the "footprint" of coastal plain development to less than 2,000 acres of the 19-million-acre refuge.

We have the pipeline in place to get the oil to market. We have the procedures and technology to protect both caribou and polar bears and we have the experience of nearly 30 years of operations in the High Arctic that prove we can produce oil without harm to the environment.

Alaskans care deeply about our environment. Some 75 percent of Alaskans would not support Arctic oil development if we did not know it could be done safely without damage to the environment and wildlife that we cherish.

Jacob Adams, a North Slope Eskimo leader, speaks about why Alaskans favor Arctic oil development. He says:

"I love life in the Arctic. But it is harsh, expensive and for many, short. My people want decent homes, electricity and education. We do not want to be undisturbed. Undisturbed means abandoned. It means sod huts and deprivation."

Conclusion:

Before I take questions let me simply say that this country needs a workable national energy policy. It needs to promote energy conservation and alternative fuels to reduce our demand for energy, but it also needs to increase supply by producing more energy domestically from public lands, be they the Arctic coast or the Overthrust Belt of the American West.

We need to have the courage to craft a truly balanced energy plan. That is what will be best for this country in the future. Thank you.

Remarks at the Annual Meeting of the Associated Press[4]

Dick Cheney

Vice President of the United States, 2001– ; born in Lincoln, NE, January 30, 1941, and raised in Casper, WY; B.A. (1965) and M.A. (1966) University of Wyoming; Nixon Administration, 1969–74, serving at Cost of Living Council, Office of Economic Opportunity, and within the White House; transition team and Deputy Assistant to President Gerald Ford, 1974; Assistant to President Ford and White House Chief of Staff, 1975–77; U.S. House of Representatives from Wyoming, 1977–88; chairman, Republican Policy Committee, 1981–87; chairman, House Republican Conference, 1987; House Minority Whip, 1988; U.S. Secretary of Defense, 1989–93, directing Operation Just Cause in Panama and Operation Desert Storm in the Middle East; awarded the Presidential Medal of Freedom, 1991.

Editors' introduction: Founded in 1848, the Associated Press is the oldest and largest news organization in the world, serving as a source of news, photos, graphics, audio, and video to all parts of the globe for more than one billion people a day. In addressing the membership of the Associated Press at its annual meeting luncheon, Vice President Dick Cheney contended that "the crisis we face" in energy "is largely the result of short-sighted domestic policies, or . . . no policy at all."

Dick Cheney's speech: Thank you very much. It's good to be here. We meet at the hundred-day mark of a new administration, one I've been very proud to be part of. The Oval Office is the final point of decision in our government, and the President has shown himself to be the kind of person you want sitting there. He's a man of conviction and discipline, who in a very short time has managed to change the tone of the discourse in Washington. He knows how to put a strong executive team in place, and has done so. And he has not hesitated to take on issues that haven't been seriously addressed in years.

One of those issues will be my topic this afternoon, and when I finish I'll be happy to take your questions.

During our campaign, then-Governor Bush and I spoke of energy as a storm cloud forming over the economy. America's reliance on energy, and fossil fuels in particular, has lately taken on an urgency not felt since the late 1970s. A few years ago, many people had

---

4. Delivered in Toronto, Canada, on April 30, 2001.

never heard the term "rolling blackout." Now everybody in California knows the term all too well. And the rest of America is starting to wonder when these rolling blackouts might roll over them.

It's only reasonable for Americans to ask if California is once again foretelling a national trend. Throughout the country, we've seen sharp increases in fuel prices, from home heating oil to gasoline, which has again soared over the past several weeks, hitting two dollars a gallon in downtown Chicago. In parts of the Northeast, communities face the possibility of electricity shortages this summer. Energy costs as a share of household expenses have been rising, and families are really feeling the pinch.

So, too, are farms and factories, which ordinarily would pass the cost along to consumers. Instead, some are simply curtailing production and laying off workers. Such costs are hard to measure in an economy as great as ours, but they do add up. By one estimate, rising fuel prices cost the economy at least a hundred billion dollars in 1999 alone.

The crisis we face is largely the result of short-sighted domestic policies, or, as in recent years, no policy at all.

The crisis we face is largely the result of short-sighted domestic policies, or, as in recent years, no policy at all.

As a country, we have demanded more and more energy. But we have not brought online the supplies needed to meet that demand. That is the problem in California, where demand has grown five times faster than supply over the last five years. And without a clear, coherent energy strategy for the nation, all Americans could one day go through what Californians are experiencing now, or worse. Such a strategy requires a hard look at the country's needs, and what is required, in supplies and infrastructure, to meet demand.

The situation has been years in the making. It will take years to overcome. But President Bush and I have begun that work.

In January, he directed me to form a task force to recommend a new national energy strategy. We will present our report in a few weeks time. You can expect a mix of new legislation, executive action, and private initiatives. There will be many recommendations, some obvious, some more complicated. But they will all arise from three basic principles.

First, our strategy will be comprehensive in approach, and long term in outlook. By comprehensive, I mean just that, a realistic assessment of where we are, where we need to go, and what it will take. By long-term, I mean none of the usual quick fixes, which in the field of energy never fix anything. Price controls, tapping strategic reserves, creating new federal agencies, if these were any solution, we'd have resolved the problems a long time ago.

Some things about the future, we cannot know. Years down the road, alternative fuels may become a great deal more plentiful. But we are not yet in any position to stake our economy and our own way of life on that possibility. For now, we must take the facts as they are. Whatever our hopes for developing alternative sources and for conserving energy, the reality is that fossil fuels supply virtually a hundred percent of our transportation needs, and an overwhelming share of our electricity requirements. For years down the road, this will continue to be true.

We know that in the next two decades, our country's demand for oil will grow by a third. Yet we are producing less oil today, 39 percent less, than we were in 1970. We make up the difference with imports, relying ever more on the good graces of foreign suppliers. How dependent have we become? Think of this: during the Arab oil embargo of the '70s, 36 percent of our oil came from abroad. Today it's 56 percent, growing steadily, and under the current trend is set to reach 64 percent less than two decades from now.

Here's what we know about natural gas. By 2020, our demand will rise by two-thirds. This is a plentiful, clean-burning fuel, and we're producing and using more of it than ever. What we have not done is build all of the needed infrastructure to carry it from the source to the user.

Then there is the energy we take most for granted, electricity. We all speak of the new economy and its marvels, sometimes forgetting that it all runs on electricity. And overall demand for electric power is expected to rise by 43 percent over the next 20 years.

So this is where we are with the demand for oil and gas and electricity. The options left to us are limited and they are clear.

For the oil we need, unless we choose to accept our growing dependence on foreign suppliers, and all that goes with that, we must increase domestic production from known sources. We must also increase our refining capacity to prevent the kind of bottlenecks that cause gasoline prices to spike in different parts of the country. As matters stand, it's been about 20 years since a large refinery was built in the United States.

For the natural gas we need, we must lay more pipelines, at least 38,000 miles more, as well as many thousands of miles of added distribution lines to bring natural gas into our homes and workplaces.

For the electricity we need, we must be ambitious. Transmission grids stand in need of repair, upgrading, and expansion. Demand for electricity is vast, but it also varies from place to place and from season to season. An expanded grid system would allow us to meet demand as it arises, sending power to where it's needed from where it's not. If we put these connections in place, we'll go a long way toward avoiding future blackouts.

That will only work, of course, if we're generating enough power in the first place. Over the next 20 years, just meeting projected demand will require between 1300 and 1900 new power plants. That averages out to more than one new plant per week, every week, for 20 years running.

It's time to get moving, and here again, we must take the facts as they are. Coal is still the most plentiful source of affordable energy in this country, and it is by far the primary source of electric power generation. This will be the case for years to come.

We can explore for energy, we can produce energy and use it, and we can do so with a decent regard for the natural environment.

To try and tell ourselves otherwise is to deny blunt reality.

Coal is not the cleanest source of energy, and we must support efforts to improve clean-coal technology to soften its impact on the environment. That leads me to the second principle of our energy strategy: good stewardship.

We will insist on protecting and enhancing the environment, showing consideration for the air and natural lands and watersheds of our country.

This will require overcoming what is for some a cherished myth, that energy production and the environment must always involve competing values. We can explore for energy, we can produce energy and use it, and we can do so with a decent regard for the natural environment.

Alaska is the best case in point. As President Ronald Reagan once said, "No one wants to treat this last American frontier as we treated the first." President Bush and I see it the same way, and so do the American people. If we had to make do with the drilling technology of the past, then there would be a strong case against exploration in the Alaskan wild.

But oil drilling has changed enormously, especially in very recent years. Three-dimensional seismic readings now have pinpoint accuracy, greatly improving the success rate and minimizing the occurrence of dry holes. In Prudhoe Bay, the vast majority of drilling over the past decade has been horizontal, allowing much oil production to go literally unnoticed, and habitat undisturbed.

The same sensitivity, and the same methods, would be applied in the event we opened production in the Arctic National Wildlife Reserve. ANWR covers 19 million acres, roughly the size of South Carolina. The amount of land affected by oil production would be 2000 acres, less than one-fifth the size of Dulles Airport. The notion that somehow developing the resources in ANWR requires a vast despoiling of the environment is provably false. This is one reason why the overwhelming majority of people who live in Alaska support developing this resource in their home state.

President Bush and I are westerners. I grew up in Wyoming, where my Dad worked in soil conservation. It's a region where stewardship is a serious matter. People rely on the land, not only for the livelihood it yields, but for the life it offers. You come to appreciate the wonders of creation all around you. The quickest way to lose respect in my part of the country is to act harshly or selfishly toward the natural world and its inhabitants. There is no excuse for that kind of reckless disregard of nature's claims. Our energy strategy will leave no room for it.

> *Conservation may be a sign of personal virtue, but it is not a sufficient basis for a sound, comprehensive energy policy.*

We can also safeguard the environment by making greater use of the cleanest methods of power generation we know. We have, after all, mastered one form of technology that causes zero emissions of greenhouse gases, and that is nuclear power. Fortunately for the environment, one-fifth of our electricity is nuclear-generated. But the government has not granted a single new nuclear power permit in more than 20 years, and many existing plants are expected to shut down. If we're serious about environmental protection, then we must seriously question the wisdom of backing away from what is, as a matter of record, a safe, clean, and very plentiful energy source.

The same can be said of hydroelectric power. Nine percent of electricity generated in America comes from dams. We must be mindful of the fish and wildlife affected by man made dams, and we can do that without placing unnecessary burdens on a very viable and safe source of energy.

Another part of our energy future is power from renewable sources, some known, others perhaps still to be discovered. There's been progress in the use of biomass, geothermal, wind, and solar energy. Twenty years from now, with continued advances in R&D, we can reasonably expect renewables to meet three times the share of energy needs they meet today, from two percent of the national total, to six percent.

The third and final principle of our energy strategy is to make better use, through the latest technology, of what we take from the earth. I've already mentioned clean-coal technology and alternative clean energy sources. But it's more than a matter of cleaner use, it's efficient use as well.

Here we aim to continue a path of uninterrupted progress in many fields. We have millions of fuel-efficient cars, where silicon chips effectively tune the engine between every firing of a spark plug. The latest computer screens use a fraction of the power needed in older models. Low-power technology has been perfected for many portable and wireless devices. Everything from light bulbs to appliances to video equipment is far more energy-efficient than ever before. New technologies are proving that we can save energy without sacrificing our standard of living and we're going to encourage it in every way possible.

In doing all these things, however, we must be clear about our purposes. The aim here is efficiency, not austerity. We all remember the energy crisis of the 1970s, when people in positions of responsibility complained that Americans just used too much energy.

Well, it's a good thing to conserve energy in our daily lives, and probably all of us can think of ways to do so. We can certainly think of ways that other people can conserve energy. And therein lies a temptation for policymakers, the impulse to begin telling Americans that we live too well, and, to recall a '70s phrase, that we've got to "do more with less." Already some groups are suggesting that government step in to force Americans to consume less energy, as if we could simply conserve or ration our way out of the situation we're in.

To speak exclusively of conservation is to duck the tough issues. Conservation may be a sign of personal virtue, but it is not a sufficient basis for a sound, comprehensive energy policy. People work very hard to get where they are. And the hardest working are the least likely to go around squandering energy, or anything else that costs them money. Our strategy will recognize that the present crisis does not represent a failing of the American people.

America's energy challenges are serious, but they are not perplexing. We know what needs to be done. We've always had the ability. We still have the resources. And, as of one hundred days ago, we once again have the leadership.

Thank you very much.

A Vision of Tomorrow, a Plan for Today[5]

Jeffrey S. Merrifield

Commissioner of the United States Nuclear Regulatory Commission, 1998– ; born in Westerly, RI, October 28, 1963; B.A., Tufts University, 1985; J.D., Georgetown University Law Center, 1992; legislative assistant to Senator George Humphrey, 1987–90; legislative assistant to Senator Robert Smith, 1990–92; associate of Washington, D.C., law firm of McKenna and Cuneo, 1992–95; Majority Counsel and Staff Director to the Senate Subcommittee on Superfund, Waste Control and Risk Assessment, 1995–98.

Editors' introduction: Commissioner Jeffrey S. Merrifield addressed approximately 850 people at the Thirteenth Annual Regulatory Conference sponsored by the U.S. Nuclear Regulatory Commission (NRC), in the Presidential Ballroom of the Capital Hilton Hotel. The Regulatory Information Conference is a forum for discussion of current nuclear regulatory issues. Attending this conference were a variety of individuals, from representatives from the nuclear power industry to members of the media and universities. In his speech, Commissioner Merrifield cautioned that the NRC must take all necessary steps to ensure that it is prepared to adequately review any new plant license, without compromising present initiatives aimed at maintaining the safety of the existing fleet of nuclear reactors.

Jeffrey S. Merrifield's speech: This is a very interesting and challenging time to be a nuclear regulator. Over the last year, there has been an increasingly louder drumbeat amongst both members of Congress and key industry leaders about the possibility of building new nuclear power plants in the United States. Of course, we at the NRC must remain agnostic about the merits of building new plants, but we cannot be caught unprepared. The NRC will have an enormous responsibility not only to ensure that tomorrow's technology is safe, but also to effectively communicate the results of our work to stakeholders on both sides of the nuclear debate.

Dean Rusk, the former Secretary of State, once said that, "unless we can find some way to keep our sights on tomorrow, we cannot expect to be in touch with today." For the NRC, our health and safety mission is too important to risk being "out of touch" on any

---

5. Delivered in Washington, D.C., on March 14, 2001, at 5:00 p.m. Reprinted with permission of Jeffrey S. Merrifield.

nuclear matter. If legislative proposals and industry discussions are any indication, the next year or two may well bring an application for a new nuclear power plant using new technology, which the NRC may presently be unprepared to review. The possibility that the NRC may not be ready today is understandable given the fact that we have not received a new plant order for decades. Nonetheless, it would be utterly irresponsible for us to remain unprepared. Therefore, we are taking steps to understand our weaknesses and future needs to ensure that we are ready for the challenges of any future plant order.

Changing Political Climate on Energy

Let me begin with some recent legislative proposals that I believe demonstrate a changing political environment for nuclear energy in the United States. Currently in Congress, there are many new or continuing initiatives aimed at enhancing the possibility that nuclear power can be a competitive, viable source of energy production in the United States. While no individual proposal provides direct funding for building a new nuclear power plant, in combination they illustrate a significant attempt to ensure that nuclear power is given serious consideration in the near future. The fact that such sweeping proposals are being considered may signal that a Rip Van Winkle-like awakening of the United States to the prospect of new nuclear power plants may be imminent.

Leading the movement for energy reform, President George W. Bush has stated that it is essential for America to have in place an energy policy that keeps power prices affordable, reduces our dependence on foreign oil, and does so in an environmentally responsible manner. Similarly, leaders in Congress are insisting that the national energy policy include prospects for new nuclear generation. Most notably, on February 26th, the Chairman of the Senate Energy and Natural Resources Committee, Senator Frank Murkowski (R-Alaska) along with Senator John Breaux (D-LA.), introduced broad-based legislation aimed at increasing domestic nuclear, oil, and natural gas generation to decrease America's dependence on foreign oil.

As for nuclear power, the Murkowski-Breaux bill, which is referred to as the National Energy Security Act of 2001, S. 388, provides for "nuclear energy production incentives" that encourage increased nuclear generation by providing up to $2 million per year for up to 15 years, to those nuclear operators that increase their generation over the previous year's output. This legislation also contains $25 million in funding for a "nuclear technology development program," to create "a roadmap to design and develop a new nuclear energy facility in the United States" and $60 million to fund nuclear research initiatives. While it is unclear what portion of this legislation will become law, it seems certain that the bill will spark serious debate in Congress about the future of nuclear energy in the United States.

Senator Pete Domenici (R-N.M.), Chairman of the Senate Appropriations Energy and Water Development Subcommittee, introduced his own energy proposal on March 9th. Unlike the Murkowski-Breaux legislation, which focuses on a wide-range of power generation issues, Senator Domenici's bill, referred to as the Nuclear Energy Electricity Assurance Act of 2001, S.472, focuses exclusively on nuclear energy.

Senator Domenici asserts that his bill is "squarely aimed" at avoiding the risk of inadequate future energy supplies. In a statement accompanying the bill, Senator Domenici stated that the United States can not afford to lose its supply of nuclear energy unless it is confident that it has a replacement energy technology that, as he puts it, offers "comparable safety, reliability, low cost, and environmental attributes." For these reasons, Senator Domenici believes his legislation will help ensure that nuclear power remains a viable energy source. Among many initiatives, the bill specifically "encourages construction of new plants." It also supports research and development of new technologies and supports the development of a regulatory framework within the NRC to ensure that new plants can be licensed.

Finally, Senator Jeff Bingaman (D-N.M.), in February introduced legislation that also focuses exclusively on nuclear energy issues. His bill, referred to as the Department of Energy University Nuclear Science and Engineering Act, S.242, is aimed at remedying an issue that impacts the NRC and industry alike; the declining trend of college graduates in the nuclear science and engineering fields. Like Senator Bingaman, I believe this is an extremely important issue that deserves the attention of Congress. The NRC cannot maintain its current regulatory programs, let alone deal with the possible review of a new plant order, if it cannot maintain its nuclear expertise. Senator Bingaman's proposal, which would authorize funding for the Department of Energy to institute programs to attract undergraduates and faculty into the nuclear field by supporting training and research in nuclear science, could assist in arresting the recent decline in new graduates.

To me, the tone and number of bills that have been introduced in such a short time demonstrate that the political landscape has shifted with respect to nuclear power. Although many members of Congress will undoubtedly remain skeptical about the increased use of nuclear energy, it seems likely that the national energy debate that will occur this year will most certainly include some of the most active discussions about the potential future use of nuclear power since the TMI accident. Because funding for any new nuclear initiatives will serve to encourage licensing requests, we at the NRC are keeping a close eye on these developments. It will be up to the President and Congress to make the ultimate policy choices about whether to encourage the use of nuclear power to meet future energy needs. Our task will be to ensure that we are prepared to review the safety issues raised by new licensing requests, should any of the bills pass and should industry move ahead and order new nuclear plants.

Industry Plans for a New U.S. Reactor

Turning to the issue of industry initiatives, it seems clear to me that the changing political climate will undoubtedly influence industry plans that were already underway for a new reactor in the United States. The NRC has been aware for months that a handful of utilities are seriously exploring the option of building new nuclear plants in the United States. In August 2000, Joe Colvin, the President and CEO of the Nuclear Energy Institute (NEI), told a gathering in London that a new plant may be ordered in the United States within five years, but that conditions for doing so may be ready in as little as two years.

A handful of utilities are seriously exploring the option of building new nuclear plants in the United States.

As you know, the NRC has already certified three new reactor designs pursuant to Part 52. These designs include General Electric's advanced boiling water reactor, Westinghouse's AP-600 and Combustion Engineering's System 80+. Because the NRC has certified these designs, I believe it is likely that a new plant order would use one of these approved designs. However, the staff is also conducting a preliminary review associated with the Westinghouse AP-1000.

Exelon Corporation has also kept the Commission informed about its investment in a project for a new gas-cooled Pebble Bed Modular Reactor in South Africa. Clearly, the Pebble Bed reactor raises a variety of technical questions. Its use in this country will depend on resolving a range of technical and policy issues, and of course, the results of the South-African initiative. If the Pebble Bed reactor proves successful in South Africa, there is little doubt in my mind that Corbin McNeil, the CEO of Exelon, will attempt to utilize this technology in the United States. Likewise, Paul Miskin, CEO of BNFL, a co-investor in the Pebble Bed reactor, recently speculated at a nuclear waste conference in Tucson, Arizona, that construction of a Pebble Bed reactor in South Africa could begin within a year and that several could be under construction in the United States within five years.

> *In many parts of the country, supply simply cannot keep up with demand.*

While even Joe Colvin viewed his prediction in August as optimistic, the recent changes in the political climate combined with the factors that originally led NEI and others to predict the new plant orders in the first place, signal that new plant orders may indeed be on the horizon. Among these factors are the following: first, the cost of natural gas and oil has soared in recent years, making nuclear power more cost competitive. NEI, relying on data compiled by the Utility Data Institute, asserts that nuclear energy was the least expensive generating source in the year 1999. Second, interest rates are considerably lower today than they were in the late 1970s and 1980s when utilities were financing the present fleet of nuclear reactors and when double digit inflation led to many plant orders being canceled. Third, more strenuous emission restrictions under the Clean Air Act have significantly impacted non-nuclear generating sources, such as coal. Fourth, the NRC has demonstrated a strong commitment to providing regulatory predictability and has significantly improved its timeliness over the last five years. Fifth and finally, there is an increasing demand for baseload power in the U.S., and in many parts of the country, supply simply cannot keep up with demand.

Obviously, the energy crisis in California has raised public awareness about energy supply issues. While it is fortunate that power shortages and unaffordable energy prices are not a problem for most Americans, the extensive news coverage of California's deep deficit of supply, which led to rolling black-outs and soaring energy prices, has awakened America to the reality that new generating capacity of whatever source must be built expeditiously, not just in California, but in many areas around the country.

This is not to suggest that I am aware of, or that I am encouraging any concrete plans for a new plant order. However, given the increasingly stronger indicators that a new plant order may be imminent, I believe the NRC must give very serious consideration to the possibility that new nuclear plant orders may become a reality in the near future.

Is NRC's Infrastructure Prepared to Handle a New Reactor License?

A new plant license application will obviously place a significant responsibility on the NRC. To be prepared for a new reactor application, the agency must have a strong infrastructure to continue to regulate the safety of existing reactors, while at the same time meeting the health and safety challenges that a new reactor application would bring. Having read the news reports of significant industry interest in new plant construction, I issued a memorandum to my fellow Commissioners (COMJSM-00-0003) this past October. In it, I expressed my view that in light of the magnitude of the technical, licensing, and inspection challenges that would be associated with these initiatives, it would be prudent for us to take steps to ensure that our staff is prepared to carry out our duty to evaluate proposed plant applications should they materialize. This proposal was not intended to promote new plant orders. Instead, it recognizes that the NRC would be irresponsible if it stuck its head in the sand and ignored reality.

My memorandum recommended that the Executive Director of Operations (EDO) take several actions to aid the Commission in understanding the steps necessary to ensure that we would be ready to meet the challenge of any new license application. These included assessing our staff's technical capabilities, inspection resources and expertise, the infrastructure supporting our construction permit and operating license regulations, and our understanding of new reactor technology. I am pleased that the entire Commission took the proposal and our responsibilities in this area very seriously. With all five Commissioners in agreement, we directed the staff to examine our readiness for a new reactor application.

In its Staff Requirements Memorandum dated February 9, 2001, the Commission directed the staff to assess the technical, licensing and inspection capabilities that would be necessary to review an application for an early site permit, a license application, or construction permit. This effort includes designs for generation 3+ or generation 4 light water reactors including the AP-1000, the Pebble Bed Modular Reactor, and the International Reactor Innovative and Secure (IRIS) designs. The Staff was also directed to examine our regulations relating to license applications, 10 C.F.R. Parts 50 and 52, and to identify whether any enhancements are necessary. The Commission recognized the need to prepare for early public and other stakeholder interaction to identify policy issues associated with using new technology and building new facilities and directed staff to thoroughly examine these issues. As for timing on the completion of these tasks, the Commission expects the staff later this spring to establish specific milestones for completing these assessments.

In sum, I believe that when the staff finishes its assessment, the Commission will have a better understanding of whether our regulations are adequate to support review of new licensing initiatives, whether our staff is technically qualified to conduct adequate reviews of the applications, and the number of staff and resources that would be necessary to effectively and efficiently review a new reactor application, should one land on our doorstep.

Impacts on the NRC from a New License

The Staff has just begun to assess the impacts of a new plant order on our agency and our readiness to address them. Obviously, I do not have the benefit of that analysis. I can, however, identify many areas that I will be using to evaluate our readiness for a new plant order.

At this point, many questions remain unanswered. For example, from a programmatic perspective, I would want to know:

- Does the NRC have the inspection capabilities necessary to oversee the construction of a new plant, given that it has been many years since we have been called upon to do so?

- Does the NRC have sufficient expertise to review a construction permit and operating license application?

- Is our research program strong enough to address the many technical challenges that could arise from using new technology or new plant designs?

In the area of policy and regulatory impacts, I would want to know:

- Can the Commission accept a reactor design that has no containment, such as the Pebble Bed?

- Will there be unique ownership and management arrangements that will have to be considered?

- Are the quality assurance regulations sufficient to assure that new parts and fuel are protective of health and safety?

- What changes to our regulations are necessary to license non-light water reactor designs such as the Pebble Bed?

- If an increasing number of non-domestic vendors are used, are our regulations applicable to import/export licensing adequate?

- How many licensed operators and how large a security force should we require at plants with new designs?

From a technical perspective, I would want to know:

- Do we have the technical capability to review advanced reactor designs and new technology?

- Do we have the expertise to review new fuel designs and technology?

- Do we have the expertise to review the numerous materials issues we will face, including those associated with the ceramics used in the Pebble Bed reactor?

- What expertise is necessary to address spent fuel disposition issues for new reactor designs?

- Do we have the codes and expertise necessary to evaluate issues related to thermal hydraulics?

- Do we have sufficient capability to evaluate an expanded use of digital instrumentation and controls?

We must provide adequate forums for the public to communicate with us so that their concerns are well understood and raised as early as possible in the licensing process.

Even if the staff has appropriate answers to these questions, I would also question whether the NRC's programs for interacting with the public are prepared for future challenges. The Commission has a significant responsibility to provide fair and meaningful opportunities for public involvement in our licensing proceedings. The Atomic Energy Act requires the Commission to offer an opportunity for a hearing to any interested person, and the National Environmental Policy Act requires significant public interaction. A new license application will likely spark a lively public debate, and our program offices will have to be adequately staffed and trained to handle these issues fairly, effectively, and meaningfully. Similarly, we must have a sound communications initiative. Most importantly, we must clearly articulate the basis for our technical conclusions. We must provide adequate forums for the public to communicate with us so that their concerns are well understood and raised as early as possible in the licensing process, and we need to have a reliable and user friendly electronic database of NRC documents.

Clearly articulating a message in a manner that avoids criticism is likely to be illusory for a regulatory agency. Yet, I am convinced that we absolutely cannot succeed as an effective regulator if we underestimate the importance of good communication. Failures in communication often cause misperceptions and cost the agency time and money to remedy. With expectations shifting in the nuclear field, and new challenges likely to come our way, we cannot afford to make such costly mistakes. Though we will never be able to please everyone, and some say the mark of a good regulator is one that is equally criticized by public interest groups and industry alike, at least we should ensure that our message is clear. To accomplish this task we need a well qualified, dynamic staff that is capable of communicating with varied and diverse communities.

Planning and Budgeting for A New Reactor Application

We need to plan and budget for the impacts on the NRC from a new plant order. Certainly, it is possible that a new plant order may not come, or may not come for many years in the future. But, we at the NRC do not have the luxury of waiting around to see whether the plans for a new plant come to fruition, before we start preparing for the possibility. While we will play no role in whether a plant will be ordered, we have to be prepared to request funding to lessen the impacts on important and demanding ongoing agency initiatives. Frankly, our most important stakeholders, the public, will demand no less than a nuclear regulatory agency that they believe is capable of understanding and judging whether new plant orders are safe.

To meet this expectation, we will need additional funding for adequate staffing levels, sufficient salaries to recruit and retain qualified staff and resources to support advanced training programs and research projects. Yet, we are already in the 2003 budget planning stage and have only just begun to assess the needs of the agency if a new license application were received. Like it or not, the NRC may very well need supplemental resources to meet those demands, if plant orders do materialize.

The issue concerning staffing is not just a budget issue. While I believe our expertise is excellent for today's licensing issues, we are facing significant staffing challenges in the near future, especially if the number of licensing issues significantly increases or the type of issues significantly changes. Just as the NRC mirrored downsizing of the industry in the last decade, the universities mirrored the same trend. Universities are experiencing declining enrollment in nuclear studies, and universities in turn, are offering fewer nuclear courses and downsizing their on-campus nuclear technology. It is unclear what effect a new plant order will have on the job market. Its possible that the optimistic attitudes of Congress and industry toward new nuclear generation may spark new interest in the nuclear field and create a larger pipeline of graduates to fill future employment needs. It is also possible that it may not.

Ensuring that we have a sufficient number of qualified experts cannot wait until the last minute. At this time our goal is to retain as many of our technically qualified staff as possible and to use creative, innovative hiring techniques to attract new, qualified employees. Our first task is to continue to identify the areas of expertise that are needed and to target universities that include studies in these fields. I know that all of the members of the Commission are maintaining an active interest in this issue. For my part, I recently undertook a recruitment effort at the University of Maryland to encourage students to join our agency. I was heartened by the excitement shown by these college students, but I was also awakened to the doubts shown by the University administrators as to the future of nuclear power. We need to continue to examine ways to convince students that oversight of nuclear reactors is exciting and challenging work. A lot will also depend on the commitment that NEI and its members make in ensuring that our nation's nuclear engineering programs remain financially viable. As you can see, there is much work to be done in the area of staffing and any successful regulatory program will require adequate planning and resources to address these issues.

> *We need to continue to examine ways to convince students that oversight of nuclear reactors is exciting and challenging work.*

Important Ongoing NRC Initiatives

Undoubtedly, it will be a significant challenge for this agency to ensure that our review of any new plant application does not interfere with important ongoing initiatives. As we prepare for the potential next generation of reactors, we must not lose our focus on the critical demands of the existing fleet and activities that we have initiated to improve our regulation of them. The dual challenge of regulating both the existing fleet as well as any new plant is one that I believe we can meet, if we take appropriate steps now to prepare our regulatory infrastructure and our staff for the challenge. To put this effort into perspective, let me describe a few ongoing agency initiatives that I believe are extremely important and which I believe cannot be compromised.

1. I feel very strongly that fundamental reforms are necessary in the area of plant security oversight. I do not know of any stakeholder that is satisfied with the NRC's current approach to this matter. In particular, there needs to be more precise guidance on the knowledge and attributes possessed by adversaries, and the difference between our regulations' reference to "enemies of the United States" and other adversaries that licensees are required to protect against. The Commission needs to bring discipline to the process of modifying security requirements in response to new information about adversary characteristics. Finally, we must bring greater clarity to the enforcement provi-

sions associated with security. I am simply not willing to allow ongoing initiatives aimed at these reforms to fall victim to competing demands.

2. I am not satisfied with the NRC's current approach to fire protection at nuclear power plants. The staff, the industry, the National Fire Protection Association (NFPA), and other stakeholders have spent significant time and resources developing a risk informed fire protection standard; NFPA 805. What do we have to show for it—very little. We have a new alternative standard that NEI informs us no licensee is willing to adopt. I am not willing to let NFPA 805 die on the vine, and neither should our stakeholders.

3. We must not lose our momentum to fine tune our new reactor oversight process. The new oversight process is a measurable improvement over our previous regulatory approach—it is a success story. However, further improvement is necessary. For example, we have repeatedly been informed about possible unintended consequences of certain performance indicators that could be adverse to safety. It would be utterly irresponsible to ignore these matters and lose possible insights by failing to examine the consequences in a timely manner or by failing to make prudent changes to the process.

4. I believe we have already lost momentum in risk informing 10 C.F.R. Part 50. Progress on Option 2 initiatives has been very slow and the gulf between the industry's and NRC's positions appears to be growing. NEI recently told the NRC staff to "fish or cut bait," when it comes to Option 2. It is time for the Commission to show more leadership in this important area. We cannot allow this initiative, which is aimed at enhancing safety by encouraging licensees to focus on the most risk significant issues, to stagnate.

5. Finally, we cannot rest on the successes that we have had reviewing license renewal applications up to now. License renewals are not, and should never become, routine. The challenges in this area are becoming increasingly rigorous as Surry, North Anna, McGuire, Catawba and Peach Bottom are on the horizon. It would be irresponsible at this point for the Commission to shortchange the resources devoted to license renewals or dilute the leadership and management dedicated to it. I assure you, I will oppose any initiative which I believe undermines our efforts in this area.

As we shift our attention to the possibility of new plant orders, we cannot neglect the growing demands of the existing fleet. I am not willing to let any of these initiatives die on the vine. I am absolutely committed to doing my part to ensure that the agency creates an infrastructure that is able to handle both important ongoing agency initiatives and the challenges that any new plant application would bring.

Industry Preparations

The industry, for its part, must recognize the enormity of the task for this agency to review a new plant order, and the advanced planning and budgeting that will be necessary. To this end, in the Staff Requirements Memorandum issued in February, the Commission directed the staff to encourage industry to be as specific as possible about its plans and schedules to enable the Commission to plan and budget for advanced reactor reviews without disrupting current initiatives. While the industry is increasingly relying on the NRC to make "just in time" regulatory decisions, our ability to handle this higher level of expectation will be significantly impacted by new plant orders.

The NRC must have adequate time and receive adequate funding to maintain its current regulatory programs and to handle the responsibilities of a new reactor license application. Otherwise, current regulatory initiatives may be compromised, milestones for licensing actions such as license renewals will have to be revisited and potentially lengthened, and review of any new reactor license will necessarily take longer. The NRC has taken significant initiatives to improve its regulatory process in the last few years, which will undoubtedly make us better prepared to review any new plant license application. But, any organization that is understaffed or underfunded, cannot accomplish monumental tasks. Consider also that the public will never accept a review that seems rushed simply to meet industry needs. The schedule must be sufficient to allow the public to be confident that our review was thorough and complete. Therefore, if industry is serious about pursuing a new plant order, it is imperative that it provide the NRC with ample time to plan for and review an application.

Conclusion

I began my discussions today talking about Congressional and industry interest in new plant construction because unlike accusations leveled against the NRC in the past, this Commissioner and this Commission do not have our heads in the sand. This is not to suggest that we are meeting the possibility of new plant construction with boundless enthusiasm. That is not our job. We are instead approaching the possibility with prudent caution. Any new plant license application will create significant challenges for our agency, and at this time we may well be unprepared for such a challenge. We will have tremendous need for scientific, technical, legal, and public policy expertise. We are facing a wave of retirements of our most seasoned and qualified personnel, yet, fewer students are entering the nuclear field to fill this void. Our communication efforts will have to support a public that is unfamiliar with the details of a new age of nuclear power plant design and construction. In the midst of any new licensing request, we will continue to be responsible for the safety of the present fleet of nuclear plants and materials licensees and the regulatory demands that they will place on the agency. Significantly, despite the expenditure of billions of dollars, the issue of permanent high level waste disposal is in no way settled.

There is no doubt that a new plant application would have a profound impact on our agency and our country. We are not and cannot remain isolated in this effort.

Thanks for joining me today. I left a few minutes remaining to open the floor for questions.

Index